O'HABITS

O'HABITS:

40 Success Habits of Oprah Winfrey and
the One Bad Habit She Needs to Stop!

WARREN CASSELL

New York

O'Habits
40 Successful Habits of Oprah Winfrey and the One Bad Habit She Needs to Stop!

Cover Design by: Rachel Lopez
Rachel@r2cdesign.com

ISBN 978-1-60037-741-9 (Paperback)

ISBN 978-1-60037-783-9 (Hard Cover)

Library of Congress Control Number: 2010920115

Morgan James Publishing
1225 Franklin Ave., STE 325
Garden City, NY 11530-1693
Toll Free 800-485-4943
www.MorganJamesPublishing.com

Habitat for Humanity
Peninsula
Building Partner

In an effort to support local communities, raise awareness and funds, Morgan James Publishing donates one percent of all book sales for the life of each book to Habitat for Humanity. Get involved today, visit www.HelpHabitatForHumanity.org.

This book is dedicated to the following persons:

First, to my wife Cleo and children Warren II, Anjanique and Chloe;

Then to all my friends and especially Beresford Mack who I know will hold me accountable should I fail to exhibit the said habits;

And finally to Oprah: Your life has been a series of lessons for me. I have learnt and now I am teaching. Thanks for being an inspiration.

Table of Contents

ACKNOWLEDGEMENTS

Writing this book was fun, believe me. I looked forward to staying up late to read and put my thoughts on paper as I studied the habits of a woman I admire so much and have been wanting to meet for the past several years. The task was not a one-man endeavor. First, I have always said that this book was divinely inspired. It's then fitting that I thank God the Father, Son and Holy Spirit for giving me the idea, strength, resources and making the divine connections that enabled me to land a publishing deal.

Then, I would like to thank my wonderful wife Cleo, for not only making the first edits, but for also putting up with my ramblings about the book. Thanks to my son Warren Jr. and daughter Anjanique who assumed the role of "Assistants", sorting the research material and all the Oprah magazines that assisted me in gleaning Oprah's success habits. Thanks also to my parents and my sisters who encouraged me from Maryland and offered support in several ways. Thanks also to my assistant Dennissia Gerald who is probably saying to herself "Finally!!!!"

Thanks to my business partner and bona fide friend Beresford Mack who saw the vision for this book the minute I shared it with him and he supported the endeavor.

To my Lawyer Leon "Chaku" Symister, thank you for your professional guidance and for constantly reminding me that "*men who are born to be hung cannot drown*".

Thanks to Shirley Spycalla, Dr. Sheron Burns and Gracelyn Cassell who read my manuscript, gave comments and made suggestions. Thanks to Karen Allen who formatted the manuscript and to Jane Grell who made the final edits.

Thanks to Arielle Ford for introducing me to Meg McAllister. And thanks to Meg for putting me in touch with the wonderful people at Morgan James Publishing and for providing excellent service as a publicist. You are truly the best publicist in the World! Thanks also to Rick Frishman and David Hancock for accepting the manuscript and placing confidence in it, and to Lyza Poulin and everyone else at Morgan James Publishing.

Thanks to my spiritual director, Rommel Lawrence who always had an encouraging word and who always reminded me to "give God ALL the glory!". I am also grateful to Verna Brandt who is like a mother to me and encouraged me to complete this book.

Special thanks to Ernestine Cassell, Dieje Daly, Shauna Harley and Idabelle Meade who gave me all of their past issues of the Oprah Magazine from which I was able to glean the habits of Oprah. Thanks also to Alphonsus "Arrow" Cassell, Sheron Burns and Nerissa Golden who bought current issues whenever they travelled (since the magazine cannot be obtained on Montserrat).

Heartfelt thanks to my inner circle of friends such as Mary Gerald, Meredith Lynch, Victor James Jr., Siobhan O'Garro, Deryll Hughes, Ivenia Benjamin, Kevin West, Donaldson Romeo, Stanford Ryan and Dawn Davis who stood with me through my most difficult times even while many others took flight. I want to say thanks to Claude Gerald who made it his business to call me and give me positive words of encouragement which allowed me to suppress the negative energy and to press on with my book during what was the most trying time of my life. To the other persons who contributed in some way and I may have forgotten to mention – Thanks.

Lastly, and certainly by no means least, thanks to Oprah for inspiring me. Little did you know that you would impact the life of a young man on a tiny island called Montserrat. I have followed your progress and studied your meteoric rise for the past twenty years. In doing so, I have learnt a lot that has assisted me to be a better person and in turn inspire others to become more meaningful citizens in society.

INTRODUCTION

The story behind the birth of this divinely inspired book is interesting. For several years, I admired Oprah and wanted to build an empire like hers in the Caribbean. For years I wrote to her and got no response and was about to have a chance to meet her.

After years of trying to contact her, my intention from the outset was not to write this book but to get Oprah to appear on my television show. I got an idea (which I believed had to come from God) for a reality show and wanted Oprah to be in it. I also wanted her to appear on my television show – "The Warren Cassell Show". I flew to Hollywood from Montserrat and got a producer to agree that he will produce the reality show if I could secure Oprah's appearance. I had already been studying Oprah and following her progress for the past seventeen years. I felt I knew everything about this woman and her support staff to the point where securing her appearance was no problem. I sent her, her best friend Gayle and her assistants and producers flowers everyday for a week just to get their attention. Then one day I received a letter from her publicist stating that she was unable to participate given her heavy schedule. I was devastated. Hundreds of persons would kill to get the attention of a Hollywood producer and I had one yet I needed Oprah.

I subsequently went to visit my parents in Maryland. The minute I decided to let go of securing the appearance of Oprah for my show and come to grips with the fact that I was not going to meet her, the idea came. At about 2am or thereabouts I heard a voice say in a clear audible manner: "O'Habits: 40 Success Habits of Oprah Winfrey…" That was a light bulb moment. If she was not going to be on the show, I could at least share what I had learnt about her over the years. At that point, I decided to buy every single book written about her and realized that most had written a biographical account of her life. I found only one which attempted to show her traits and even that one was in my opinion lacking.

I flew back to Montserrat and began gathering every single article she had written in her magazine and stormed the library on my little island seeking to devour every single article written by and about her. I solicited past issues of O The Oprah Magazine from friends and relatives. I watched shows and made notes as her words supplied me with the evidence of the habits I dubbed "O'Habits".

I now have a sense of joy because I have in some way contributed to the movement of making others live a better life.

Part 1

A Word on Habits

Watch your thoughts, for they become words. Watch your words, for they become actions. Watch your actions for they become habits. Watch your habits for they become character. Watch your character for they become your destiny.

—Unknown

First we make our habits, then our habits make us.

—Charles C. Noble

I am writing this chapter on the first day of January 2009. It's a time when I normally get my goal book and write down my goals and resolutions for the next twelve months. Each year, I resolve to be a better person and form better habits. Unfortunately, by March of each year I totally renege on my resolutions. However, I think I am in a better position this year given that I have done extensive research on the issue of forming better habits and especially since I have identified at least 40 of Oprah Winfrey's that I can emulate. I am also resolved to be mindful of the things I want to accomplish this year. If we agree with Tracy's notion of a habit, that is, "*95 percent of everything that you think, feel, do and achieve is the result of habit.*", [1] then I think it's safe to say that I will begin to feel, think and achieve my desires.

Joel Olsteen defines habit as "*an acquired, learned behavior that we do without even thinking about it.*"[2] Some are obviously good and some are bad. Having discovered most of Oprah's good habits, one question arose. Can you really become a creature of new habits? I believe you can and the sorry one-liner "it's a hard habit to break!" is nothing but an excuse for refusing to take control. Janet Rae Dupree believes that:

> *Rather than dismissing ourselves as unchangeable creatures of habit, we can instead direct our own change by consciously developing new habits. In fact the more things we try – the more we step outside our comfort zone – the more inherently creative we become, both in the workplace and in our personal lives.*[3]

The good news: habits are learnable if we make that conscious effort. I once read that children can be potty trained in one day by providing them with lots of liquid and taking them to the toilet whenever you think that their bladder is full. Tracy says that "*the speed of new habit pattern development is largely determined by the intensity of the emotion that accompanies the decision to begin acting in a particular way.*"[4] Using the desire to lose weight as an example, he says that it is a common desire that most fail to achieve. However, whenever their physician says that they will die if they do not lose weight, then the thought of dying becomes so intense or frightening that the individual immediately changes his or her diet and starts exercising.

The experts say that a habit can be broken in 6 weeks while Tracy says that a habit pattern of medium complexity can be formed in 21 days. The key is to quit feeding the bad habit and start nourishing the good ones. The irony is that we are fully aware that "good" habits will produce good and healthy lifestyles. So why do we continue to practice those bad habits? Dr. Phil suggests that we "*cannot eliminate our negative behavior without understanding why we do it to begin with.*" He says:

> *If you are engaging in some behavior or pattern of behavior you must assume that no matter how strange or illogical it may seem, you are engaging in it in order to create some result that you want. Whether you want it or not, you do*[5]

I would also like to add that we tend to cling to poor habits because they keep us in our comfort zone and keep us away from change and adventure!

After watching Oprah, reading her articles and listening to her interviews over the past fifteen years, I've managed to identify 40 of her good habits (which I have dubbed O'Habits) that I believe have catapulted her to the level of success she now enjoys. Some of them are simple but effective in making us more productive and successful people and as such, I urge you to systemically adopt some if not all of the O'Habits in the following chapters. As this book is not only about Oprah, but also about you becoming a better person, I am giving the habits a human connection. After all, if Oprah can do it so can you and in the next chapter I will tell you why she's an excellent example to follow.

Why 40?

W hen I was divinely inspired to write this book, I had no idea why I decided to list 40 habits as opposed to 10, 20 or 30. In fact, I did not at that time realize that 40 was extremely significant. As time passed, I then became convinced that this book must have been divinely inspired since the significance of the number forty was revealed to me.

The number 40 has a good relationship with the fulfillment of promises. Todd Dennis and Richard Anthony blog that "*Of all the types and shadows of the Old Testament, none is as pervasive and important as the shadows revealed in the relationship between "forty", and the fulfillment of promises.*"[6] It's almost as if "40" is preparatory for transformation. Consider the fact that the normal period of pregnancy is 40 weeks, after which a living creature slides (literally) into the earth. Elijah had one meal that strengthened him for the next 40 days (1Kings 19:8), and 40 stripes was the maximum whipping penalty according to Deuteronomy 34:7.

Rick Warren in his famous work "The Purpose Driven Life" writes that "*The Bible is clear that God considers 40 days a spiritually significant time period. Whenever God wanted to prepare someone for his purpose, he took 40 days.*"[7] He then made reference to Noah whose life was transformed by 40 days of rain, Moses who gained much courage and confidence to become a dynamic leader after spending 40 days on Mount Sinai and Jesus who became empowered after 40 days of fasting in the wilderness.

Arthur Blessing, whose story recently made it to the big screen in the movie "The Cross" carried the cross throughout every single country in the world over a forty year period. There is just something about the number 40.

I am therefore proposing that the following 40 "O'Habits" be digested over the next forty days while seeking to adopt as many as possible into our own lives. It's hard to disagree with Rick Warren who says that "[o]ne reason most books don't transform us is that we are so eager to read the next chapter, we don't pause and take time to seriously consider what we have just read. We rush to the next truth without reflecting on what we have learned."[8] This book, therefore, is not a book to be read overnight, but rather, one should read and digest it one bite-sized chapter per day with a view to becoming a better person.

It is my desire that after the 40 days of reading this book, you would have adopted most if not all of the O'Habits with a view to understanding that these same habits are determining factors in attaining the goals you've set for yourself. Finally, I also hope that this book reaches the New York Times best seller's list and stays there for at least 40 weeks.

Why Oprah Winfrey?

No matter what you're selling, there's no greater single guarantee of success than getting yourself booked on Oprah.

Time Magazine, May 9, 2007

At this point, you're probably asking "why the habits of Oprah?" as opposed to Ellen Degeneres, Donald Trump, Martha Stewart or Tyra Banks. Well, first of all, it's a lot easier to glean the habits of Oprah without meeting her, because apart from her show, she writes about herself every month in her magazine – "O The Oprah Magazine". And not only does she have a lot of material out there, she is also very candid. She opens herself up to us in the hope that we too search within and find our true selves and for that, her influence in my opinion is second to none. Moreover, Oprah has decided that she will end her talk show after being on the air for twenty-five years. This book sums up what there is to learn from "the most influential woman in the world".

In its December 2007 issue, the Hollywood Reporter in paying tribute to Oprah as its "Leadership in Hollywood Honoree" stated that her "influence had grown to rival that of the White House and maybe to be even greater in people's hearts and minds."[9] No one dares debate that after all the worldwide attention, her meteoric rise has caused even the naysayers to throw in the towel. With a number one talk show for over 20 years, this multiple Emmy winner, who decided to remove her name from the list since no one else was winning, has a penchant for causing unknown authors to become best sellers literally overnight. Oprah is success personified.

Everything she touches turns to prophetic gold. Her influence transcends generations. She is a woman that has seen wave after wave after wave of struggles but has overcome time and time again to be the success story that she is today. As a result, she constantly speaks about those good habits that have made her who she is today. "O'Habits" examines such habits and encourages readers to adopt them in order to accelerate the process of prosperity and success in their own lives.

Brian Tracy, one of America's foremost authorities on developing peak performance and individual achievements, notes that "the most important discovery in the field of psychology and success is that fully 95 percent of everything that you think, feel, do and achieve is the result of habit. Beginning in childhood, you have developed a series of conditioned responses that lead you to react automatically and unthinkingly in almost every situation."[10]

I wanted to examine what has made Oprah as successful as she is and why no other talk-show host in the United States has been as influential as she is. I often wonder why some people were successful and others were not. Some seemed blessed and some seemed very much cursed. While writing this chapter and in fact just before writing this paragraph, I was summoned by telephone to the local police station, only to find that a young man was arrested and charged for burglary. He had been arrested at least five times prior to that and swore he was going to keep out of trouble. I represented him in court before and could not believe that he had committed another similar offence. On the other hand there are others, who, like Oprah, enjoy nothing but success after success.

Is Oprah's success a matter of being at the right place at the right time? Her influence is undeniably tremendous. CNN and Time.com called her "arguably the world's most powerful woman"; The American Spectator called her "arguably the most influential woman in the world"; Time Magazine called her "one of the 100 people who most influenced the 20th Century" and "one of the most influential people" of 2004, 2005, 2006 and 2007. She is the only person in the world to have made all five lists. Her personality is engaging and people like to read about her. So, on that note, let us not only examine her habits but also let us aim to emulate them. Everybody knows Oprah and these are her habits!

Part 2

O'Habit #1: Oprah Goes to Bed Early and Rises Early

Early to bed early to rise makes a man healthy, wealthy and wise.

Benjamin Franklin

In her "What I know for sure" column in the September 2006 issue of Oprah Magazine she writes that *"every sunrise is like a new page, a chance to receive each day in all its glory."* Going to bed early and rising early is a habit that Oprah employs and is one that we should practice as well. If you watch the Oprah show or read the magazine, you would have heard her say that by 8:30/9:00 pm she's in bed to be up by 5:00 am. This seems to be consistent with the favored quote *"early to bed early to rise makes a man healthy, wealthy and wise"*. But does it really matter whether you go to bed early and rise early?

Brian Tracy in his book "Million Dollar Habits" says that

"When you get up early, at 5:30 or 6:00 in the morning, you will have ample time to think about the day ahead

and to plan your work activities. Early rising gives you
an opportunity to read, reflect, and meditate. Early rising
enables you to get up and going without a feeling of pressure
to rush out of the house in order to get to work on time[11]

Oprah knows that and goes to bed early, looking forward to the beauty and the opportunities of the morning. There is just something inspiring about the morning that people who sleep through the morning seem to miss. Henry Ward Beecher believed that "the first hour is the rudder of the day."

Going to bed early also puts us in sync with nature. In former years when electricity was not invented, people relied on God's natural light and went to bed just past sun down and got up before sunrise. This allowed them to diligently pursue their daily goals knowing that there were no hundred watt bulbs to facilitate them in the night hours. This practice seemed to facilitate our bodies' natural rhythm and gave our bodies the right amount of rest. Nowadays, we go all day and all night because we feel we have the ability to produce light. Construction sites have night shifts and sporting events are hosted in night under the brightest of lights. Little do we realize that the depression and overweight we sometimes experience may be caused by improper sleep patterns. We should therefore strive to go to bed early and rise early. It's no coincidence that going to bed early is married to rising early. Rising early without going to bed early would mean depriving your body of the rest it is designed to have on a daily basis.

There are also spiritual reasons why some get up early in the morning. For Evangelists like Kimberly Daniels and Cindy Trimm, "God is an early riser" and hence we too should be early risers. Cindy in her book "Commanding the Morning" cites several examples of prophets and saints who rose early to pray or hear God's voice. Kimberly Daniels is convinced that your destiny is wrapped up in the fourth watch which is between 3am - 6am. Affirmations said during this time will manifest themselves in the earth realm when day breaks.

Whether it is for spiritual reasons or just to plan your day and meditate on the work that lies ahead, we should make it our business to, like Oprah, go to bed early and rise early.

Tips for Practicing O'Habit #1 – Going to bed early and rising early:

- Go to bed at the same time everyday and early unless you cannot avoid it. For those who think they cannot get to bed before midnight, try completing your task before 7pm. Pack the children's school bags and iron your clothes for the next day as soon as you come home;

- Try to avoid stressful activity just before going to bed. Do not exercise just before going to bed. In fact you should perhaps read or listen to something pleasant before going to bed. Avoid watching news just before bed as it is normally riddled with depressing and frightening information;

- Use your bedroom only for sleeping and avoid taking work related matters there;

- Let all your friends and associates know that you will not be available after the time which you have set as bedtime.

O'Habit #2: Oprah is Loyal

Lack of loyalty is one of the major causes of failure in every walk of life.

Napoleon Hill (1883 -1970)

Do not let loyalty and faithfulness forsake you; Bind them around your neck and write them on the tablet of your heart.

Proverbs 3:3

According to Dr. Mike Murdock, "*disloyalty is an invisible, silent, and often unnoticed decision by someone close to you to destroy your dream and participate in your downfall*".[12] In this dog-eat-dog world we live in, and in a world where most believe and think that "it's all about me!", Oprah's loyalty is a trait that has helped her attain the success she now enjoys. She is loyal and she expects loyalty from her staff, friends and those with whom she has a relationship. This loyalty is a significant contributing factor to the long-serving handful of executives that stood by her side for the past several years. Harpo's president Tim Bennett says:

She has always been first and foremost loyal to her partners...
Several years ago, she was offered tens of millions more by a

competing network to go with their stations. It was a lot
more money than we were being offered by ABC. But at the
end of the day, Oprah stuck with ABC, because that is where
she got her start and she believed in the relationship she had
with those people.[13]

Her loyalty is also seen by the fact that after much national
success, she turned down invitations to move the show to LA,
stating that she was loyal and grateful to the city of Chicago from
where she went national. To this day, as cold as Chicago is in
winter, the Oprah Winfrey show is recorded there and will remain
there for the duration of the show's life all because of loyalty.

Oprah not only expects loyalty but seems to demand it
by virtue of an iron-clad confidentiality agreement that each
employee is expected to sign. A person who is loyal will always
put his friendship above money, values and morals above lust,
and obedience to the word of God above gratifying the flesh.

Remember King David in the Bible. It was disloyalty that
allowed him to disregard the morals and sleep with his soldier's
wife. On the other hand Joseph's loyalty toward his master
Potiphar caused him to run from his master's wife after she
had invited him to sleep with her. Such loyalty caused him his
freedom. Yet he declared:

As long as I am here, my master does not concern himself
with anything in the house, but has entrusted to me all he
owns. He wields no more authority in this house than I do,
and he has withheld from me nothing but yourself, since you
are his wife. How then could I commit so great a wrong and
thus stand condemned before God?

Joseph was loyal to his master. People who are disloyal have no morals and are oftentimes jealous. Sometimes therefore the disloyalty stems from jealousy, that is to say that some of the people you work with and perhaps know well may very well be jealous of your achievements. As a result they begin to sow discord among other employees. Beware of those who attempt to be close to you only to destroy you. Donald Trump believes that "*one of the problems when you become successful is that jealousy and envy inevitably follows*". These jealous people will always be disloyal. Let's resolve like Oprah to make loyalty a trait and to also demand it of others before it is too late. We should also refuse to tolerate disloyalty.

Dr. Mike Murdock says that one of the biggest mistakes of his entire life "has been to tolerate harmful people too long. Disloyalty is not like a common cold. You cannot take two aspirins and go to bed. Disloyalty is more like a cancer racing throughout your body."[14]

Tips for Practicing O'Habit #2 – Loyalty:

- Let your employees, employers, friends and associates know that you are loyal and you expect loyalty;

- Where necessary get a confidentiality agreement signed so as to encourage loyalty;

- Dismiss immediately any disloyal persons in your midst.

O'Habit #3: Oprah Gives

Give and it will be given unto you full measure pressed down, shaken together and running over will be poured into your bosom for with the measure you use, it will measure to you.

Luke 6:38

No man has ever been honored for what he received. Honor has been the reward for what he gave.

Calvin Coolidge

WHEN YOU LEARN, TEACH, WHEN YOU GET, GIVE. Maya Angelou taught me that.

Oprah Winfrey

In the November 2004 issue of the Oprah Magazine, Oprah wrote:

We've all heard that it's more blessed to give than to receive. Well I know for sure that it's also a lot more fun. Nothing makes me happier than a gift well given and joyfully received. [15]

Unlike most of us, Oprah does not just say so, she has lived by every word of it. Giving is another success habit of Oprah.

Whether it's two hundred and seventy-six cars to members of the Oprah Winfrey Show audience, a house as a wedding gift to a staff member or as she says just "*mailing a thoughtful, handwritten note to someone who didn't expect it.…It doesn't matter what the thing is; what matters is how much of yourself goes into the giving, so that when the gift is gone, the spirit of you lingers.*"[16]

There's no doubt, that Oprah's selfless giving not only lingers in the hearts of those who receive it, but in those who hear and talk about her giving as well.

In 1997, Oprah created the world's largest piggy bank which by the end of that show's season banked $3.5 million. Normally when we put our loose change in a piggy bank, we do so hoping to treat ourselves in some way. However, that piggy bank was not for Oprah, nor her organization, it was for the purpose of blessing others. That money gave fifty (50) students a chance to attend college.

And who can forget the coveted 276 car give away! Yet after giving away the 276 cars to the audience members she said "…it's the most fun I've ever had during a season premiere… even now when I think of the shrills of pure joy I heard on the show that day my own heart rises all over again."[17]- What an unexpected response. One will not truly experience this joy unless he/she learns to give, and give without inhibitions.

Throughout her life we witness that she is most joyful when she gives. That's a concept I myself had to re-program my mind to accept. While doing my Masters of Law degree in San Francisco, California in 2002/2003 I experienced the fullness of that joy when I was prompted to give away a foot long Subway teriyaki sandwich and an orange juice. I had just bought the treat after a few hours of classes and was on my way home. I stopped by the Catholic Cathedral on Mission Street and there was a homeless man who I would see on a daily basis just sitting in church two pews in front of me. I heard a voice, though only audible to my spirit say "give what you've bought to that man".

I was a student on a budget, so a teriyaki sandwich wasn't an everyday delight or give away for me. "Give and go without" the voice said. I obeyed and the joy that came from that act was more satisfying than biting into that sweetly glazed foot-long teriyaki sandwich.

To top it all off a few hours after arriving home, I received an email from a law firm in California seeking to register a few trademarks on Montserrat which would bring me much needed money. This venture was exactly what I needed. I was blessed in many ways that day. As a result of giving, I experienced the joy of giving and receiving.

Giving is the only way to demonstrate that you've conquered greed. Everything that God has given to us continues to give after it has been given. The sun gives light, the trees give oxygen and the earth itself provides several raw materials such as oil and natural gas which are so critical to our survival. No wonder Oprah feels "life isn't about what you can have; it's about what you have to give."[18]

John Mason, author of bestseller "An Enemy called Average" concurs by adding that "*If you are dissatisfied with your lot in life*", you should "*...build a service station on it*".[19] Oprah has indeed built not one but several service stations on her lots. The Oprah Winfrey Foundation and the Angel Network Foundation are examples of such service stations. Through these organizations, she has donated more than $50 million to charity.

In December 2002, Oprah went to South Africa presenting 50,000 children with a plethora of gifts. "It was the best Christmas I've ever had" she says. When she built the Oprah

Winfrey Leadership Academy for Girls in South Africa she flew to Africa to personally select the first seventy-five students. She originally donated $10 million to the school, but her spirit of giving is seen in the fact that her donation to such a school has exceeded $40 million.

Further, in preparing the school's design she was told that most of the students were not accustomed to much and that the '*simplest environment would be a luxury to them*'. How many times have we fallen into this trap by giving something we ourselves would not be happy in receiving. The "it's not good enough for me but it's good enough for someone else" mentality is not at all a trait of Oprah. She sent back the mediocre plans saying "*I said, from the start, I am creating everything in this school that I would have wanted for myself - so the girls will have the absolute best that my imagination can offer.*"[20] When we give we should always give the best. The act of giving these girls an opportunity to better their lives through education was so satisfying, she remarked "it's the first time in my life that I've said I feel proud of myself."

There is no doubt that when we give we feel better. The late Mother Theresa once warned that "unless life is lived for others, it is not worthwhile. A self-centered life is totally empty." Best-selling author Joel Olsteen writes that "*God created us to be givers. And you will never be truly fulfilled as a human being until you learn the simple secret of how to give your life away.*"[21]

Oprah's reality show is evidence of this. Of all the reality shows on television, none has impressed me more than "Oprah's Big Give". Why? Because most reality shows are about contestants vying for an end that is of benefit to themselves. The men on "I Love New York" supposedly get a chance to hook up with New York, the winner on Survivor gets a million dollars, and on "Next Top Model", the winner gets $100,000 and a modeling deal.

However, the contestants on "Oprah's Big Give" had no idea that the winner would take home $500,000 in addition to $500,000 to give away as he or she pleased. They were only told that they would have to give big while being away from their home and families for several weeks. Throughout the show the contestants basked in the tremendous joy of giving while those who received seemed to be so touched as the adage "it is more blessed to give than to receive" gained significance in their lives. No other reality show has motivated viewers to do something that would enhance other people's lives.

Oprah is truly a big giver and it's that O'Habit that keeps her cup running over. She is more satisfied however, with the non-tangible results of her giving. "*The enjoyment comes from knowing the receiver understands the spirit of the gift. I make an effort to do something good for somebody everyday, whether I know that person or not.*"[22] Just think, maybe one of those girls from Oprah's Academy, in recognizing the gift Oprah has given her, will want to help change Africa for the better in the future.

Tips for Practicing O'Habit #3 – Giving:

- During spring cleaning if you find stuff you have not used in a year, give it away. Joel Olsteen says "*If it's not meeting a need turn it into a seed.*";

- Skip a meal once a week and find someone needy to give. Try to ensure it's someone who you may never see again. Do not expect anything in return from that person;

- When at the shopping counter at a supermarket, pay for the person ahead of you. I tried that the other day and was once again overtaken by the feeling of joy;

- Give out of your own neediness. Often times we tell ourselves that we cannot give because we ourselves need. I've found that when I was in need and gave, I was abundantly blessed;

- Give your best and do not give grudgingly.

O'Habit #4: Oprah wears Integrity on her Sleeve

If you have integrity, nothing else matters. If you don't have integrity, nothing else matters.

Alan K. Simpson

You must consider the bottom line, but make it integrity before profits.

Denis Waitley

President of Harpo Productions Inc. Tim Bennett says that Oprah *"..has incredible energy and her integrity she wears on her sleeve."*[23] She is honest and desires to do right not just to one but to all. Oprah attributes her integrity to something bigger than herself *"I am guided by a higher calling. It's not so much a voice as it is a feeling."*[24]

Part of being a person of integrity is about giving your word and keeping it. In a world where a man's word is replaced by detailed written contracts and escrow agreements, Oprah's word is like gold bricks. In an interview with Hollywood Reporter's Christy Grosz and Stephen Galloway she said:

*...if I tell you I'm going to do something, even if it means
flying all night to do it... – I [was] committed to do[ing]
something for Quincy Jones in Rome, and (as) time got closer
I really was just overwhelmed, and it was just going to be
impossible for me to get to Rome. But I did it! I flew to
Rome. I was on stage for 46 seconds and got on the plane
and flew back.*[25]

Integrity is not only sticking to promises made, but it is also
about telling the truth. In the Bible we read about people being
stoned to death if they lied. Nowadays, people lie on resumés,
in interviews and to their spouses without any feeling of guilt.
Integrity then is fast becoming an uncommon trait.

For Oprah, being truthful helps her live her best life. For
instance the mad cow trial she was involved in was all about her
simply saying that news about the disease stopped her dead in
her tracks from eating beef. Oprah was being truthful in her
comments and was dragged over hot coals by the media and beef
industry moguls for her integrity, which clearly shows us that
people may not necessarily want to hear the truth all of the time.
However, Oprah feels that telling the truth is her responsibility:

*I personally have the responsibility to tell the truth. But
truth in real life or TV is not necessarily the truth in a court
of law. There are a myriad of ways to interpret an event or
an experience. You can tell the truth without having to tell
the whole truth. And we believe in the truth...* [26]

In 1994 the movie "Interview with a Vampire" was released
and Oprah, who was to interview Tom Cruise about the movie,
was unable to see the video before she got to California. When
she eventually saw the film she hated it. In fact, she said she

had "*an abysmal reaction to it! It felt dark and oppressive to me.*" Notwithstanding that this was two hours before taping she called Tom's publicist to tell him that she did not like it. She found it impossible to go on television and promote something that she was uncomfortable with. Now that's integrity.

In recent times we have seen law makers throughout the world passing legislation dubbed "Integrity in Public Office Act" or something of that sort. It's a bit disheartening to see how integrity is so rare that we have to be passing legislation demanding it.

However, we can learn from Oprah how to become people of integrity. Let's resolve to be honest, committed and truthful so that when we depart this earth those remaining will only have good things to say about us. For as Oprah says "*in the end, all you have is your reputation.*"- And that's something Bernard Murdoff obviously never valued.[27]

Tips for Practicing O'Habit #4 – Being a person of integrity:

- Resolve to be honest with yourself and others at all times;

- Whenever you make a commitment – Keep it!

O'Habit #5: Oprah Lives out of the Box

Whenever you find yourself on the side of the majority, it's time to pause and reflect.

Mark Twain

We've all heard the saying *"Think outside the box!"*. Well, Oprah does not only think outside the box she lives outside of it. *"I don't do things just for TV"* she says, and that has helped keep her at number one position in talk show history for several years. If you are thinking that most of the show ideas are not hers, it doesn't matter because Oprah is a team player and having the ultimate say means that she could have dismissed several of the ideas that her team mates brought. The "Book Club" is a good example. An idea advanced by Alice McGee, a producer who has been with her from the beginning. An idea that would probably have been turned down by network executives if the show was still being produced by the network for fear of dipping in the ratings. After all, how much ratings would a show about books muster. Nonetheless, Oprah ran with it, and as the story goes the face of the literary industry was changed forever. Every single book listed on Oprah's book club reached the best sellers list and stayed there for several weeks – all in the face of negative projections.

That's Oprah! She and her staff are innovative, and since she came on the airwaves in the 1980s there has been a plethora of talk shows. Notwithstanding the new shows that come on the air, none has kept our interest and has been as consistent as Oprah's. As it relates to the direction of the show she's said:

On my own I will just create, and if it works it works, and if it doesn't, I'll create something else. I don't have any limitations now on what I think I could do or be.[28]

Anyone who has seen her show knows that they have been indeed creating and creating; taking the show to higher heights and out of the talk show box where other shows and hosts reside. In 1989, she went into the delivery room and showed the world how a baby was being delivered. In 1998, she made a music video which was totally out of the realm of a talk show host. Looking back now she says "*who do I think I was?....that's clearly one of those cases where you stepped outside of yourself and you lost sight of the truth*"[29]

Other out of the box highlights have been:

- Showing up at McDonalds in 2002 to work the drive thru window and announcing that "*Today's lunch is on me!*";

- Showing up at a couples house in the night in 1993 to babysit for them so they could go out to dinner since the wife never gets to go out with her husband;

- Attending Air Assault school to undergo a part of their basic training and experience what those in the armed forces go through. Oprah at the end of it said that she now has "*greater respect for those in the armed* forces.";

- Getting her ears pierced on air.

Sometimes the out of the box thinking and living also benefits not only the viewers, but also third persons. The Angel Network for example was inspired by a little girl who managed to collect $400,000 worth of pennies and loose change. Oprah got viewers to save up their loose change to the point where millions were collected, giving scholarships and building homes for the needy, all because of spare change, an out of the box idea and the medium of television.

It is always tempting to "*not invent the wheel*" but rather to repeat what others who are successful did. Sure there are other talk shows, but the Oprah Winfrey Show stands out. On Montserrat I grew up with most people discouraging me from becoming a lawyer for several reasons, including the fact that the 39 square mile island already had several lawyers. Nonetheless, I was determined to become not only a lawyer but the Eastern Caribbean's first full time entertainment lawyer. I was inspired by a quote my mother put in my autograph book which went like this:

> *Consider the world as a mountain, look where the millions stop, there is always a crowd at the bottom....Press on! There's room at the top!*

What limitations are we putting on ourselves when we conform to the status quo? Whatever your field or calling, I challenge you to do like Oprah - think and live outside of the box. Push the boundaries and get ahead of others in the field.

Tips for Practicing O'Habit #5 – Living Out Of the Box:

- Break your pattern based way of thinking and do what you would not normally do;

- Refuse to be discouraged by people if you feel it in your gut.

O'Habit #6: Oprah Prays

Prayer is not asking. It is a longing for the soul. It is daily admission of one's weakness. It is better in prayer to have a heart without words than words without a heart.

Mahatma Gandhi

The function of prayer is not to influence God, but rather to change the nature of the one who prays.

Soren Kierkegaad

Ⓞne thing is certain, Oprah recognizes that there is a being more powerful than her, and so she constantly relies on Him for divine assistance through prayer. That makes praying yet another O'Habit:

My prayer to God every morning on my knees is that the power that is in the universe should use my life as a vessel, or a vehicle, for its work. Prayer, that's the central thing for me.[30]

And throughout her shows, you can hear her saying things like "*I prayed that…*", or "*My prayer is that…*". I cannot recall another talk show host admitting or even mentioning prayer on the air or publicly without any fear of criticism and believe me I've watched them all. In fact, I recalled that prior to the September 11 event, it was almost politically incorrect to mention God and prayer lest those who did not believe in a supreme being be offended. However after the event I was amazed to see every major network carrying services where denominations of all kinds came together to remember those who had passed and also to pray. You see when all else fails prayer will bring us through. Charles L. Allen believes that and writes of people who refuse to bring their hopes, dreams, fears and desires to God that "*The trouble with many people is that they are so big in their own eyes they feel no need of God.*"

On November 20, 2009, when Oprah announced that she was going to bring down the curtains on her show in 2011, she informed viewers that she was doing this "*after much prayer*". This demonstrated how important prayer was in making such a decision. She surely did not need to continue the show, yet she was humble enough to seek the divine direction showing that if it did not settle well in her spirit she would continue.

While some consider prayer as a time to rattle off to God their wish list, Oprah prays through every kind of situation. Even in her generosity she prays. When she gave away the 276 cars to commence the 19th season she said:

> *I wanted the force of the gift to be about not just the cars but the essence of what it means to share what I have. I prayed for that, sitting in the dark with my shoes and handbags. Then I walked downstairs to the studio, and pandemonium hit. Delight at a thousand decibels! My prayers were answered: Everybody felt blessed.* [31]

When life gets to be overwhelming, when you feel like the tasks you have are bigger than you, or even just in experiencing the joy of a moment, surrender it to God in prayer like Oprah and let this be a constant habit. Let us acknowledge Him in all our ways and our paths will be directed.

Tips for Practicing O'Habit #6 – Praying:

- Set aside a time in the morning to pray and spend quality time with God. It should be the first thing you do upon rising;

- Keep praying throughout the day;

- Listen for direction.

O'Habit #7: Oprah Laughs

We don't stop laughing because we grow old; we grow old because we stop laughing.

Michael Pritchard

One must laugh before one is happy, or one may die without laughing at all.

Jean De La Bruvere

According to an Irish Proverb, "*A good laugh and a long sleep are the two best cures*". And while the proverb never said what exactly a good laugh will cure, we can only assume that it will cure ailments of all sorts. Oprah is one who surely loves a good laugh, even if it means being a part of practical joke. "*Who would have thought I'm a practical Jokester?*" asked Oprah as she with the help of Jeremy Kennedy, pulled a practical joke on an unsuspecting viewer who thought she had won a competition to spend a day with Oprah. It was all in the name of getting a good laugh and by the end of the episode Oprah and viewers were laughing non-stop. You see, Oprah loves a good laugh and even took the time to devoting more time to shows just to let viewers laugh because she and her producers "*believe in having more fun".*[32] In one show, Jeremy Kennedy gave a guest a very bad make-over as a practical joke and had Oprah and viewers in stitches. Never before had I seen Oprah asking viewers at the beginning of the show to *"call your friends because this is very funny".*[33]

There is nothing worse than being in the presence of a sour puss! Trust me I've been there and you could be in a group of 7 people and not have a good laugh because of the energy of one sour puss. I therefore avoid people who are uptight, complainers and cannot enjoy a good laugh. Oprah believed that her make-up artist Reggie Wells, was the "biggest complainer" she had known. What cure did she recommend for him? Oprah sent him to classes with the American School of Laughter's founder and Director Sebastian Gendry. The result was amazing and left Reggie saying *"thank you Mr. Gendry! I walked into your laughter session very depressed. It was Easter weekend and I was very lonely. What you had me do did not just lift stress from my body, it lifted stress from my soul."*[34]

During most of her shows Oprah can be heard roaring with laughter whenever there is a funny moment. Author Richard Lederer, a blogger writes:

> *We all need to laugh. Recent studies have shown that he or she who laughs last. Norman Cousins, who used laughter to conquer a debilitating disease, writes "Illness is not a laughing matter. Perhaps it ought to be. Laughter moves your internal organs around. It enhances respiration. It is an igniter of great expectation . . . . It has always seemed to me that hearty laughter is a good way to jog internally without having to go outdoors…Laughter stimulates the circulation, tones the muscles, energizes the lungs and respiratory system, stimulates endorphins in the immune system, boosts the*

neurotransmitters needed for alertness and memory, increases motivation to learn, and provides superb aerobic exercise.[35]

Emma Bombeck who is considered one of America's funniest columnists wrote before dying *"If I could have lived my life over, I would have laughed more."* Karen Elizabeth Angus blogs that:

Laughing relaxes facial muscles that can become very tense especially on long working days. Plenty of laughter creates 'laugh lines' in a person's face, giving the person a kindly look, as opposed to wrinkles and creases caused by stress, unhappiness and hardship, which age a person and give him or her a hard and angry appearance.[36]

Laughing is truly "the best medicine" and a habit we all should adopt. Let's resolve to have a little more fun and like Oprah laugh more, because after all, "a merry heart doeth good like medicine".

Tips for Practicing O'Habit #7 – Laughing:

• Laugh, laugh and laugh.

O'Habit #8: Oprah Reads

Books for me have always been a way to escape. I now consider reading a good book a sacred indulgence, time alone to be any place I choose. It's my absolute favorite way to spend time.

Oprah Winfrey[37]

I n his best-selling book the *Purpose Driven Life*, Rick Warren says that where you are five years from now will largely be determined by the books you read. Books alter the way you think and feel about yourself. No one knows this more than Oprah who shares that:

books showed me there were possibilities in life, that there were actually people like me living in a world I could not only aspire to but attain. Reading gave me hope. For me, it was the open door.[38]

On my island, Montserrat, every year on August 1st, we celebrate the life of a man named Nincum Riley. He was a man who in the 19th century was the only slave who was able to read aloud the law that abolished slavery. Over one hundred and fifty years later he is still remembered as a hero because he was able to read. It's no surprise then that Oprah has such great regard for books and reading. She says that "*reading books is the single greatest pleasure I have.*"[39] Having learned to read at age three, Oprah says she then "*soon discovered there was a whole world to conquer that went beyond our farm in Mississippi.*"[40] If Oprah wasn't an avid reader who recognized the value of literacy, she might not have been the Oprah we know today. Reading has opened doors for her and made her want to "aspire" to "attain" more from life. Further, not only did Oprah re-shape her life and thinking through reading, she also wants to challenge us to do the same.

Reading has the ability to transform lives and Oprah wanted to facilitate such transformation by promoting reading on her television talk show. In 1996, she started a book club amidst criticism that her ratings would dip. And while ratings did dip a little, Oprah got America reading like never before! She also single-handedly placed every single book she endorsed on the best-sellers list.

One year after the launch of the book club, a guest told her "b*efore I joined the book club, I had never read an entire book.*" Oprah recounts that giving others the chance to positively change their lives through reading was "*one of my proudest moments.*"

This reshaping is continuous, and Oprah continues to show others the value of reading. She has given several young ladies the chance to make good with their lives through reading and learning. She equipped the Oprah Winfrey Leadership Academy in Africa with a library complete with plush seating around a fireplace "*so that the girls can read…*"[41] Every classroom has teaching space outside with leafy trees shading cool benches enabling the girls to "*sit with a book or be with yourself.…a reading tree!*"[42] Reading has played such a defining role in her life that she insists on using her influence, money and persuasion to do the same for these girls:

I can't imagine where I'd be or who I'd be had reading not been such a fundamental tool in my life. I wouldn't have gotten my first job in radio at age 16 which led to TV three years later. [43]

Maybe in some way Oprah sees herself in all of those little girls who were less fortunate and wants us to see that no matter what our circumstances are, we can change our situation for the better by reading.

Not only does reading boost your self-worth and value, it will better prepare you to keep up with our ever changing world. We are currently in the midst of an information explosion where we see that companies whose business is primarily the gathering and dissemination of information are worth more than other companies. Brian Tracy explains:

We live in a knowledge based, information based society. Successful people are simply those who know more than their competitors. One of your most important responsibilities is keeping up with your field, staying ahead of your pack by continually taking in more information. [44]

How do we do all of this? We have to continuously read. Tracy goes on to state that the knowledge base of any profession doubles every seven years. Imagine that! Whatever profession you are in right now, all the knowledge of that profession will be twice more than what it currently is seven years from now. This means that in seven years one would have to know twice as much just to keep up. And how do we keep up? Once again by reading. Tracy says that if one reads one hour per day within his field he will be an expert in 3-5 years, a national authority in 5 years and an international authority in 7 years.

So thank God for the gift of books and reading. It's an O'Habit that has surely helped Oprah keep ahead in her field and has allowed her to think outside the limited box, the world sometimes enfolds us in. "*Had I not been taught to read at an early age, I'd be an entirely different person. Thanks to books, I knew there was another kind of life.*"[45]

Tips for Practicing O'Habit #8 – Reading:

- Read at least one hour per day within your chosen field;

- Read to your children from an early age;

- Underline and make notes while reading, thereby personalizing the books (assuming you own the book);

- Invest 3% of your income on books, magazines and self development materials.

O'Habit #9: Oprah Treats her Staff Well

Outstanding leaders go out of their way to boost the self-esteem of their personnel. If people believe in themselves, it's amazing what they can accomplish.

Sam Walton – Founder of Wal-Mart, Inc.

In his book "Secret Service: Hidden systems that Deliver Unforgettable Customer Service" John R. Dijulis III writes that:

The one common theme among the most successful companies is that they take good care of their employees and create a strong corporate culture. If you treat your team members well, the majority of them will take good care of your clients.[46]

This can be said of Oprah and that is why one of her habits is treating her staff well. She's known for giving houses for wedding gifts, cars and other assets most people would spend a lifetime to acquire. Oprah's behavior is consistent with the survey conducted by the Council of Communication Management which says that the top motivator of employee performance is recognition for a job well done.

But treating her staff well is not a new habit of Oprah. Oprah started treating her staff well even before she began making millions. She recalls picking up sweaters and donuts for everyone at work, just because. According to Bob Nelson:

> *While money is important to employees, research shows that what motivates them really to perform - and to perform at higher levels—is the thoughtful, personal kind of recognition that signifies true appreciation for a job well done. Numerous studies have confirmed this. The motivation is all stronger if the recognition creates excitement, and enhances sense of value and respect, and a story the employee can tell to family and friends, and associates, possibly for years to come.*[47]

And boy, her staff sure has stories to tell their friends and family for years to come. The story is told of how a former personal assistant was given a small box containing a brochure for a Jeep Cherokee. Before she could ask what it was about, she heard a horn honking and looked out the window only to see another one of Oprah's aides leaning against a brand new Cherokee Jeep that was for her. Producers have received diamond earrings and luggage with a $10,000 travel gift certificate inside. One former producer Debra DiMaio is reported to have been given a year's certificate for once-a-month dinners with friends in Montreal, Paris and London with all expenses paid. In 2005 to celebrate the end of season nineteen, Oprah threw a party with a Hawaiian theme and then announced "*I am taking all of you to Hawaii!!! I'm not only flying you but I'm flying your entire family!!!*"[48]

That was not at all an isolated event. As if she wanted to top that gift, she recently showed her staff appreciation in June 2009 by taking them and their families on a 10- day cruise of the Mediterranean. Transportation, food, and activities all paid for. The trip which was also enjoyed by the employees' family members, cost over 9 million dollars and came at a time when other organizations were still cutting back on expenses due to global economic hard times. It covered Spain, Italy, Turkey, Greece and Malta. The joys of working for Oprah!

But Oprah is not alone. There are several companies with CEOs who recognize the importance of treating staff well. Take for example MBNA - a credit card company headquartered in Delaware. It offers employees aerobic classes, fitness centers, and cafes. In addition they also offer scholarships for children of employees, in house day care and tuition reimbursement. The message? Treat your staff well and the bottom line will be affected. Oprah knows that and will continue to embrace this habit. Why shouldn't we?

Tips for Practicing O'Habit #9 – Treating your staff well:

- Customize the reward to the person;

- Send even a simple email to show appreciation;

- Practice day-to-day recognition;

- Surprise your employee with a surprise day off;

- Read Bob Nelson's book: 1001 Ways to Reward Employees.

O'Habit #10: Oprah Keeps and Adores Dogs

There's no psychiatrist in the world like a puppy licking your face.

Ben Williams

The reason a dog has so many friends is that he wags his tail instead of his tongue.

Author Unknown

Appearing on the Ellen Degeneres talk show Oprah told Ellen, *"I don't understand people who don't love dogs."* Keeping a dog apparently has lots of benefits and Oprah is hardly seen without her dogs. *"They go with me everywhere,"* she told Ellen. When she started her show she was not allowed to bring her dog to work and so as she says *"I thought I'd get um....I bought my own show!"*[49]

She's been bringing her dogs to work since owning her own studio. She has been keeping dogs for a while now and may not even know that doing so helps lower high blood pressure and cholesterol according to a New York State University Study.

It's often said that a dog is a man's best friend and it's one friend that Oprah has been maintaining over the years. Keeping a dog is therefore another success habit of Oprah Winfrey. But for Oprah keeping one is not enough. She loves dogs so much she got three at one time having being *"charmed by their cute little faces, intoxicated by that sweet puppy breath and the underbite on Puppy number three (Layla)."*[50]

Even the experts believe it is a good practice. Anne Kirrin – editor for small breeds.com reports that according to Hospital studies:[51]

> *seniors and recently operated on patients responded better to treatment and got better quickly while they were in contact with dogs and other therapy animals. Just petting a dog can be relaxing and therapeutic for recovering patients. Also, owners of dogs have a greater chance to survive after suffering from a serious illness. Several studies have discovered that pet owners who suffered from a heart attack were more likely to be alive a year after they were discharged from the hospital than those who did not own pets. Another New York study found that pets affected their survival rate even more than the presence or company of family members or friends.*[52]

I believe Oprah's dogs are the most fortunate in the world. Which other dog can boast of flying (by private jet) to Hawaii or going on an exotic cruise in the Mediterranean. When one of her dogs fell ill she got so much attention and care from the vet that Oprah had to remark *"I wish for every citizen of this country the kind of healthcare and treatment this little dog received."*[53] Now that's a healthcare plan Americans would love.

And who would have thought that one of the busiest woman in showbiz would have all this time to spend with her dogs – after all it's hard work and perhaps that's what's keeping Oprah stress free. According to her:

> *I spent weeks getting up at all hours of the night with them. I picked up pounds of poop and am still in the throes of puppy training so they can have good manners. It's a lot of work. A month in, I had to hire some help because I was so sleep deprived- and trying to keep three at a time from destroying my worldly goods was making me constantly frazzled. Whoa, did I gain new respect for mothers of real babies!*

What are the other benefits of keeping dogs? It is said that dog owners are generally happier in that it reduces loneliness and fights depression in their owners. In addition dog owners can expect to live longer, given that they do not have to cope with the high stress associated with the absence of a dog. Whatever the benefits, Oprah says *"One thing I know for sure: I can't begin to repay my own dogs for the flat-out joy they bring me."*[54]

Tips for Practicing O'Habit #10 – Keeping Dogs:

- Get a dog. If it is your first time, talk to a dog owner and lover you know and begin to prepare yourself and your home for your new family addition;

- Search your local book store for books about keeping dogs. You are paying to find out information that took someone years to research. It will help you avoid mistakes.

O'Habit #11: Oprah Uses Flowers

Flowers are the sweetest things God ever made, and forgot to put a soul into.

Henry Beecher, Life Thoughts, 1858

Whether they're placed on her office desk or at her home Oprah is never too far from flowers. In fact she loves flowers so much that she built a tea house on her property in Montecito California, surrounded by hundreds of rosebushes, thousands of hydrangeas, and a sea of dahlias just to get away from it all.

Her love for flowers is magnified at the teahouse. Each flower is hand-picked by Oprah herself and boasts "...*varieties of perennials and annuals creating a natural, unplanned feeling.*"[55] The variety of roses includes Brass Band, French Lace, Sunset Celebration and the Marilyn Munroe.

As for the kind of flowers, just make sure they are real. In a 1996 show dubbed "Our best decorating ideas ever" Oprah tells us that she:

Believe that flowers were meant to be fresh. They were not meant to be fake. So plastic flowers to me are about the worst thing you could do when you call yourself having good taste.[56]

Her love for flowers is seen by the planning that went into her garden in California. Oprah secured the services of Dan Bifano who has designed several high-profile gardens, to create an entirely new breed of roses. The result was the "Legends Rose" which became available to the public in December 2008 and is said to be one of the largest hybrid teas ever created.

With all of this Oprah has a different view about flowers:

I don't think of flowers as something material. Flowers come, and then they go back to where they came from. You can't hold them for long.[57]

Oprah's genuine love for them is seen by the fact that while most spend thousands of dollars maintaining other assets that are fixed such as a vintage car or an expensive painting, she doesn't mind spending thousands on flowers even though you "*can't hold them for* long". She knows that they make a difference in our surroundings. An office with flowers adds life and lifts your spirit.

Oprah loves flowers and uses them to brighten her day, her surroundings and sometimes just to show appreciation. Perhaps she's compensating for not having a garden when she was a child.

Tips for Practicing O'Habit #11 – Using Flowers:

• Plant some flowers in your backyard and nurture them;

• Send your loved one flowers at least once per month in addition to special occasions;

• Find someone who you appreciate and send them flowers without letting them know who sent them.

O'Habit #12: Oprah Recognizes it takes a Village

If I could solve all the problems myself, I would.
Thomas Edison[58]

Do you want a collection of brilliant minds or a brilliant collection of minds?

R. Meredith Belbin

I just want to thank everybody for your countless hours sacrificing your family…I say this every year and I mean this sincerely… I understand that I do not stand alone, that it is everyone of you who stand behind me that makes the work go out in the universe and speak to millions of people….[59]

These were Oprah's words of appreciation after bringing the nineteenth season to a climax at a season finale party (before announcing that she was taking the entire staff and their family to Hawaii). How many bosses do you think will take the time out to say "thank you!" to the people who work for them sacrificing hours to make the boss look great. I'm sure

48

not many. The attitude is that the employee's salary is sufficient acknowledgement. However, Oprah is different. She realizes that she doesn't "stand alone" and it is important to thank the people who help her.

Jesus was probably the greatest man to walk this earth and in establishing His ministry, He chose a team He referred to as disciples to assist Him in spreading the gospel. Some of the greatest entrepreneurs are successful because of the team they work with. Oprah is no exception. She realized early in life that it takes a village and its efforts to attain and maintain standards that have kept her at the top.

Mike Murdock says that "*arrogance will not reach for others, but humility recognizes that others possess something you do not.*"[60] In a way Oprah shows her humility by recognizing that her empire could not have been built without the team. Dr. Myles Munroe concurs with Dr. Murdock in his book The Principles and Power of Vision: Keys to Achieving Personal and Corporate Destiny when he reminds us that:

> *We need other people if we are going to be successful in life because....we were not created to fulfill our visions alone. As a matter of fact God specifically said about His first human creation 'It is not good for the man to be alone. (Genesis 2:18). We need people to make it in life. Again, individual purpose is always fulfilled within a larger or corporate purpose. Therefore, it's important that we work with others in making our visions a reality.*[61]

Having a team is not the only thing, but putting your trust and confidence in the team is also essential. Oprah has full confidence in her team of supporters. "*I try not to micro-manage*",[62] she said in an interview explaining the 276 car give away. Not only does this demonstrate that Oprah has trust in her employees' abilities, it also shows that the employees have demonstrated that they are worthy of that trust. Who wouldn't after having such a generous boss?

There is no way Oprah could have succeeded without her team. After all, Oprah does not hold the camera, neither does she edit the video footage or write the scripts. She is the host and no matter how good a presenter she is, the show has enjoyed its huge success over the years because of the combination of efforts from every single person. Oprah knows this and will constantly declare "*It takes a village!*"

Tips for Practicing O'Habit #12 – Recognizing that it takes a village:

- Identify the various aspects of your business, find people who are good at those areas and delegate tasks to them;

- Know your limits/weaknesses and get assistance in those areas.

O'Habit #13: Oprah Always Uses Positive Words

The real art of conversation is not only to say the right thing in the right place, but to leave unsaid the wrong thing at the tempting.

Dorothy Nevil

Normally when we think about evil things men do, we think about those who drink alcohol, those who steal, those who are involved in some form of immorality, those who murder, those who violent and abuse others physically. But how often do we think about all the evil that is done through the use, or misuse, of the tongue?

AL Macias

I've never heard Oprah say something negative and I've been watching the show for the past eighteen years. And while I have not seen every single episode, I can say that Oprah's words are always seasoned with grace. Using positive words is another positive habit of hers that we should aim to adopt.

Robert Morris in his book <u>The Power of Words</u> writes that:

Words build bridges to strangers and keep existing relationships fresh. For good or ill, what we say determines the character and quality of those relationships. That's why Max De Pree, a member of Fortune Magazine's National Business Hall of Fame, and a recipient of the Business Enterprise Trust's Lifetime Achievement Award, once said, 'There may be no single thing more important in our efforts to achieve meaningful work and fulfilling relationships than to learn to practice the art of communication'.[63]

Words connect us to each other and for almost 25 years Oprah has been connecting like no other. No wonder she remains number one over the years. Moreover, the saying *"what you sow is what you reap"* proves true with Oprah. It's hard to find someone who has a bad word to say about Oprah. In fact, the first publisher I called about this book said *"we adore Oprah and if the book is negative, we're not interested!"* A book publicist said the same thing to me as well. When it comes to words you definitely get back what you give. The book of Proverbs confirms this in chapter 18 verse 20: *"a man's stomach shall be satisfied from the fruit of his mouth, and from the product of his lips he shall be filled."*

While I do not promote placing one of the O'Habits above the other, I am tempted to say that if you disregard all the other habits and keep this one, you would see the tremendous difference in your life. Dr Cindy Trimm has recorded a teaching on an audio CD dubbed "What Have You Put in the Atmosphere?" she says:

words go into dimensions that our physical bodies may never be able to go, and no matter how modern men are, men often have underestimated the power of the spoken word. Words don't just dissipate once they leave your mouth, words are permanent. Words are as permanent as your spirit. …words have life, words are prophetic , words have no geographical limitations, words transcend time and space.[64]

We hang by our tongue and knowing that, Oprah uses positive words in almost every situation. Even when she felt she was duped by James Frey, author of A Million Little Pieces she was graceful in her speech.

Robert Morris notes several symptoms of a sick tongue and having watched her show and read her "What I know For Sure" columns over the years, I believe I am qualified to determine whether she has any of the symptoms:

Symptom #1 –Telling the Untruth: Oprah is so truthful, one has to cringe sometimes at the things she shares and encourages people to share. For example, the fact that she was molested by her uncle and became pregnant by him.

Symptom #2 –Stirring Up Division: Not Oprah! She brings people together all the time.

Symptom #3 –Dishing the Dirt: Not since she decided to have "change your life TV". In fact, Oprah does not gossip or at least not on the air.

Symptom #4 –Passing Along False Information: Please? The Oprah Winfrey show and the Magazine are the personification of truth. Whenever false information may have gone out (like with James Frey), she is quick to correct it.

Symptom #5 –Breaking Confidences: Let's not even go there! Have you ever heard Oprah revealing something said to her in confidence? I know she's known for those ironclad non-disclosure agreements.

Symptom #6 –Speaking Curses Instead of Blessings: You can always tell a celebrity who curses. I can almost swear that Oprah has never used the "F" word.

Let's face it. Oprah is the Queen when it comes to talking and talking positively is what she does well. Why not adopt that habit?

Tips for Practicing O'Habit #13 – Using Positive Words:

- Go on a tongue fast for thirty days by refusing to say anything negative, slandering or discouraging, etc. Buy the book 30 Days to Taming Your Tongue by Deborah Smith Pegues. You will be happy you did;

- Pause before replying to someone you are tempted to curse;

- Live by the old saying: If you can't say anything good, don't say anything at all.

O'Habit #14: Oprah Delegates

You can delegate authority, but not responsibility.

Stephen W. Comiskey

I magine having an empire like Oprah's - comprising of two charitable arms; The Angel Network and The Oprah Winfrey Foundation; two magazines; Oprah Magazine in New York and South Africa respectively; Harpo Films in Los Angeles, a production company dubbed Harpo Inc; a school for girls thousands of miles away; and more recently a TV network called the Oprah Winfrey Network. Now imagine you are maintaining contact with every single aspect of managing those companies. The thought is enough to drive one crazy and this is why it definitely takes a village to run an empire like Oprah's. However, having "the village" is not enough; one also needs the ability to properly delegate tasks to adept people, as well as placing full confidence in them.

What exactly is delegation? It has been defined as:

division of authority and powers downwards to the subordinate. Delegation is about entrusting someone else to do parts of your job. Delegation can be defined as subdivision and sub-allocation of powers to the subordinates in order to achieve effective results.[65]

This is what Oprah did when she hired Libby Moore as Chief of Staff Personal Assistant. Libby's job is to liaise *"between Miss Winfrey and the gazillion arms of her world."*[66] By delegating that work to her, Oprah isn't as overwhelmed as someone who feels they must do it all.

An effective leader or manager delegates. Oprah is aware that if she had to do everything herself she would have burnt out pretty easily. A perfect example of Oprah at work was when we got a peek into how she runs her empire on the "A day in the Life of Oprah" feature on her 20th Anniversary collection DVD. There we saw Oprah introducing her four assistants who after walking into her make-up room were given tasks. Also, while filming the behind the scenes feature she told one of them that a letter was *"to be done this morning and you need a verification that they've received it….and after Friday I will be sending out no more invitations….that's it….that's our lockdown"*[67]. During the same feature Oprah explains that they get thousands of pieces of snail mail and thousands more of email. And according to her *"there's a whole department that just handles that"*. In fact, we see the order in her organization as she explains:

> *This is how my mail comes to me. These are high priority open request by type. So instead of me looking at all the pieces, Nirvana sits at her desk and she goes through and tells me what all the pieces of mail are and then I check off if I want to see it or not want to see.*[68]

This is definitely a reminder of a Queen Bee who is surrounded by worker bees who meet her every need. Clive Green says that:

> *With proper and effective delegation, you can have more time to focus on the things that need your attention. The important thing that you should remember is to choose the person well in*

whom you will entrust your business. Proper communication with them will help you to avoid future misunderstandings and ensure that their tasks are performed to the best of their ability.[69]

As I am writing this chapter a former head of Government comes to mind. Having been appointed to lead my country he failed to delegate. Although surrounded by competent staff, he took on almost all of the tasks he faced. He wanted to do everything himself and even refused advice when it was needed. Despite his pure intentions he was never re-appointed Chief Minister and is considered to date a failed leader. Delegating is an important habit and should be adopted to keep your sanity and stay on top of your game.

Tips for Practicing O'Habit #14 – Delegating:

- Define tasks and determine whether such tasks are suitable for delegating. Not every task should be delegated. The rule is to delegate what others are able to do while you do what only you are able to do. For example while Oprah can delegate the editing of a piece, she surely is the only person that can host the show;

- Decide the most suitable person to delegate the task to;

- Give that person a time frame and parameters with which to work. You may also tell them what you are expecting of them;

- Provide feedback after the task is over so as to ensure that the quality of work is maintained;

- Delegate some work to others so that you can make time for your spouse or partner.

O'Habit #15: Oprah Hires the Best

If your think hiring professionals is expensive, try hiring amateurs.

Unknown

The key for us, number one, has always been hiring very smart people.

Bill Gates

We have already seen how Oprah acknowledges that she could not be successful on her own. However, merely having a team is not enough and Oprah takes it a step further – she hires the best! It is that habit of hiring the best that has taken her production company Harpo from being a five-person company to a multimedia conglomerate that now hires over 450 full time staff and grosses over $400 Million dollars annually.

If we were to conduct a human resource audit I am sure we would find that it is the crème de la crème of the media industry that ends up at Harpo. The editing of the show is excellent, the graphic design of her magazine is flawless and the lighting on the set is second to none. I need not mention her hair and make up! One thing is certain – Oprah is not surrounded by amateurs.

It was the best Attorneys that advised her to buy the show from ABC in 1988 and, through a syndication agreement with King World, continued the show, generating multiple streams of revenue through distribution. It was her desire to secure the best that caused her in 1994 to re-enlist her former WLS-TV boss, Tim Bennett. Mr. Bennett had left Harpo four years earlier to manage a television station in North Carolina. Oprah knew his ability and requested that he return to assist in putting operating systems in place. He is currently serving as the President of Harpo Productions Inc.

Even outside the realm of work Oprah insists on hiring the best. In 2005 when she decided to honor her personal African-American heroines with three unforgettable days of festivities, she hired renowned event planner Colin Cowie – a man that People Magazine describes as *"the go-to-planner of choice for parties that awe even A-listers."*[70] and famed New York City Chef Jean-Georges Vongerichten. In addition, 200 waiters trained over a three-day period so that at the rolling of the drums 400 plates went down simultaneously in a moment – "Synchronized serving" I am told it is called.

Oprah is not alone when it comes to the habit of hiring the best. Legendary Automobile mogul Lee Iacocca says *"the most important thing a manager can do is hire the right new people."* This is consistent with Donald Trump's statement that *"my philosophy is always to hire the best from the* best." Ron Popeil writes that:

> *I realized a long time ago that I am not an expert in every area. That's why I work with professionals to assist me in the creation and marketing of my products. I do know what consumers like and how to market a product, but I know*

very little about engineering, about motors, and how things work internally. So I bring in professionals to work with me and have always been fortunate to surround myself with people who I always felt were a lot smarter."

Mike Murdock says that King Solomon who is known as the richest man who ever lived was also known for hiring the best. Murdock says of Solomon:

When he wanted the highest quality craftsmen in brass, Solomon sent for Hiram. In 1 Kings 7:14, Hiram is described as a man filled with wisdom and understanding and cunning to work all works in brass…Solomon loved beautiful woodwork and insisted on hiring only the best craftsmen. 1 Kings 5:6 says, 'for thou knowest that there is not among us any that can skill to hew timber like the Sidonians'.[71]

Like Oprah, let us strive to employ the best or ensure that if we are to be employed we would be described as being the best.

Tips for Practicing O'Habit #15 – Hiring the best:

• Make sure the person you hire is tried and tested;

• Get a report from at least two or three former employers;

• Refuse to tolerate employees that demonstrate inferior qualities. Dismiss them if their incompetence becomes overwhelming. It would cost you more in the long run.

O'Habit #16: Oprah is faithful to One Partner

Drink water from your own cistern, running water from your own well.

Proverbs 5:15

Let no one say when he is tempted, "I am tempted by God"; for God cannot be tempted by evil, nor does He himself tempt anyone. But each one is tempted when he is drawn away by his own desires and enticed.

James 1:13-14

I n the glamorous world of celebrities, being married three or four times or having several romantic relationships and affairs is a common thing. Nonetheless, even though Oprah has never been married, according to Helen S. Garson, Oprah stands out in that she has endured much *"pain that sexual domination brought into her life, from her teens right through her years in Baltimore when an affair with a married man brought her close to suicide"*[72]. As we will see in a subsequent O'Habit, Oprah does learn from her mistakes.

Given all that has changed in her life – her hairstyle, her weight and her revenue making potential, one thing remains constant: Her man. Over the years, she has had one partner to whom she's faithful and has remained so. This despite the fact that she admitted to **Ladies Home Journal** in 1988 *"a good man is hard to find…and the smarter you get, the harder they are to find."*[73]

When she was considering who she'd have as a partner she employed reason stating to Cosmopolitan:

He'd be taller than me, smarter than me, and not threatened by me. He'd have to be outgoing but know when to shut up. And I don't think it would matter if he was black, white or Chinese.[74]

Finally in the 80's she found a man that was consistent with her vision of the ideal man – Steadman Graham. A man who was intelligent, ambitious and handsome, and someone who was not drawn to her as a result of her fame and fortune. And while Oprah and Steadman discussed marriage in the early part of their relationship she has publicly stated that she may never get married. Yet, she remains faithful and totally dedicated to this man. Oprah attributes her first light bulb moment on relationships to her discussion on a 1988 episode with marriage therapist Harville Hendrix. After that episode Oprah says:

I saw relationships not solely as the kind of romantic pursuit our society celebrates but as a spiritual partnership that's meant to change how you see yourself and the world[75]

No one can doubt that being faithful requires dedication and hard work. Stormie Omartian agrees when she writes *"everyone gets tempted to sow outside his own garden. The ones who resist, and instead deliberately plant seeds of fidelity, reap a harvest of plenty. Even if you have the most perfect marriage ever known to man, the enemy will still try to tear down the fence and destroy it by one means or another."*[76]

There is no doubt that being faithful to one partner has its benefits having regard to the possible consequences: other STD's and drama! Yeah, imagine Steadman being threatened by Oprah's other boyfriend or the other boyfriend stalking her. That's drama Oprah can live without, in fact, drama we all can live without. Just look at what happened to Tiger Woods. His multiple affairs (which I consider to be an attempt to be a sexual athlete of Olympic standards) threatened not only his marriage but his livelihood in that popular brands cancelled endorsement deals for fear that it would tarnish their image. We also heard lots about Elizabeth Edwards and her very successful husband. Elizabeth experienced a public blow to her marriage – a marriage that she describes as a *"perfect marriage"* when speaking to Oprah in an interview for Oprah Magazine. After her husband had an affair and allegedly fathered another child Elizabeth has declared that there is a need for *"women to have more respect for other women."*[77] I would add to that and say that men too need to respect other women and even other men. I have a friend who says that if he visits a female friend who has a boyfriend or husband, he refuses to even go inside the house if his friend is not there and he expects the same of his male friends. I hope I am exempted from this rule since I am his wife's cousin.

I believe we should all think rationally before we yield to temptation. We need to pause even for a split second and think about the things that could go wrong after the unfaithful event and ask *"is it worth it?"* Only yesterday I had cause to do that and with all that's at stake I answered in the negative.

Oprah stands by her man and is faithful. If we all emulate her, this world will be a better place. Let us try even though she says:

Yes a relationship requires work. Yes it means sacrifice. Yes.
It's about compromise. But if it's healthy, it should bring
you joy not just some of the time but most of the time. And
whether you're 25 or 45, single or married, it should involve
bringing all of who you are to the table- walking away
together with even more.[78]

Tips for Practicing O'Habit #16 – Being faithful to one partner:

- Resolve to be faithful. Why leave steak at home to go out and eat corned beef;

- Communicate with your spouse the attraction you may have for someone else;

- Be honest about your feelings and tell someone to whom you will be accountable;

- Make sure the person you hire is unattractive at least to you. Creflo Dollar says he or she can be attractive but not to you.

O'Habit #17: Oprah Does Not Allow Money to Consume Her

No matter how rich you become, how famous or powerful, when you die the size of your funeral will still pretty much depend on the weather.

Michael Pritchard

Riches may enable us to confer favours but to confer them with propriety and grace requires a something that riches cannot give.

Charles Caleb Colton

W hen you think about Oprah, you can't help but think about money. One generalization we all make is that people with lots of money are usually consumed by it. One blogger writes that the best definition of wealth he has ever heard is "[t]*he number of alternatives a person can afford to buy*". While Oprah may have a lot of money so as to afford several alternatives, she surely does not allow her wealth to consume her. Another blogger puts it like this:

If [Oprah] were to give away $10,000 a day, and if her pile of capital did not generate any more capital, and if she never earned another dime on TV, it would take her 100,000 days to give it away. That's 274 years.[79]

Oftentimes we hear about a celebrity who becomes a national and international sensation and who makes millions of dollars only to lose all of it through splurging. MC Hammer comes to mind – a man who after paving the way for Hip Hop by selling in excess of twenty million copies and earning millions went broke through unnecessary spending. More recently Britney Spears has been criticized for not saving or investing any of her monthly income of $737,000.00. As for Oprah she is not moved or motivated by money declaring that *"life isn't about what you have; its about what you have to give."*[80] She has an excellent relationship with money and does not let money consume her. During the November 20, 2009 episode on which she announced she was quitting the show she said to Ray Romano *"I don't make any decision based on money (thank God) and I don't have to."*[81]

The notion that money will take care of all our problems is a rather popular one. There is a notion that the media feeds with shows like VH1's "Fabulous Life" and songs like P Diddy's *"Its all about the Benjamins".* Nonetheless Oprah remains focused on her vision to help others make a better life for themselves through the medium of television rather than the assets she could accumulate with the money she's made. She writes:

Yet for me, the path to success was never about attaining incredible wealth or celebrity. It was about the process of continually seeking to be better, to challenge myself to pursue excellence on every level. …I've learned that, yes wealth is a tool that gives you choices-but it can't compensate for a life not fully lived, and it certainly can't create a sense of peace within you[82].

And while she occasionally goes on a shopping binge that leaves us in awe (like buying a house she liked for $50 Million when it was valued for $30 Million), she can hardly be described as materialistic. Her presence is disarming and her admission to being unable to read a balance sheet makes her more the friend next door rather than a shrewd CEO. As Jennifer Harris and Elwood Watson put it:

Obviously, Winfrey is less interested in celebrating corporate know-how and power than she is in generating and managing its charitable, cultural, and educative counterpart – making money for the pleasure of giving it away.[83]

While most are driven by money, Oprah has made millions but does not let her millions consume or define her. In fact, when her show was first syndicated, she said she never doubted that the show would be popular but what she was surprised about was the amount of money it would make her. She jumped about her apartment taking pictures of her first million dollar check. Despite the rewards she confesses "*I never did it for the money. I always did it to prove myself and to show myself and to see how far I could be stretched.*"[84] Her recent decision to end the show in 2011 also shows that she is not motivated by money. After all, she raked in an estimated $275 million dollars from the show in 2008 alone. Talk about a decision that's definitely not motivated by money!

In addition to not allowing money to consume her, having made a lot of money, Oprah will not allow others to swindle her out of it either. She advises everyone and especially celebrities to *"sign your own checks."*

Whether she has money or not Oprah remains Oprah. Her life seems to echo Luke 12:15 which says *"Life does not consist of the abundance of things"*. Maintaining a good relationship with money is an O'Habit we ought to adopt. After all money does not change a person, it simply magnifies who they are.

Tips for Practicing O'Habit #17 – Maintaining a good relationship with money and not allowing money to consume you:

- Accept the fact that money does not define us;

- Give every time you get in order to conquer greed;

- Separate your needs from your wants so as to curb your appetite to splurge or emotionally spend.

O'Habit #18: Oprah Knows the Value of a Good Friend

You can always tell a real friend; when you've made a fool of yourself, he doesn't feel you've done a permanent job.

Laurence J. Peter

Your friend is the man who knows all about you, and still likes you.

Elbert Hubard

Let your acquaintances be many, but one in a thousand your confidant.

Sirach 6:6

Walter Winchell once said that "*a real friend is one who walks in when the rest of the world walks* out". Oprah has experienced this in her life through her friendship with Gayle King. She remarked that when she was about to go national with her talk show "e*verybody…except* Gayle *said I would fail*". Like many of us, Oprah casually refers to people she meets as her "friends" however Gayle is the one true friend she cherishes the most. "*What I know for sure about friendship? That Gayle King is a friend I can count on*".[85] Oprah describes their friendship as being "b*etter than a marriage or a sexual relationship.*"[86] She's the one person we have seen at Oprah's side over the past twenty-three years.

While it is good to have more than one friend, it is recommended that we should all be able to have that one person we can count on who will help us live better lives. The book of Proverbs 18:24 states *"A man of many friends comes to ruin"*. In support of the same, the book of Ecclaesiaticus commonly known as Sirach says *"let your acquaintances be many and your friend one in a thousand"*. The direction of your life is heavily determined by the friends you have. And therefore the quality of your friendship will assist in the determination of your destiny. What if Gayle had joined with the naysayers and discouraged Oprah? Oprah may not have been enjoying the success she is enjoying today; and in turn Gayle would not have been reaping the benefits of the said friendship.

Dr. James Merritt, founder of "Touching Lives" agrees and in one of his Sunday sermons said that *"There are people in hospitals this morning because they were with the wrong type of friends last night, there are teenagers in jail this morning because they were with the wrong kind of friends last night."*[87] No wonder Solomon warned in Proverbs 12:26 *"the righteous should choose his friends carefully for the way of the wicked leads them astray"*.

The destructive force of a friend is illustrated in the biblical story of David's son Amnon who raped his sister and was murdered by his brother. Such tragedies could have been avoided if Amnon's friend had advised him otherwise. The story is told in 2 Samuel 13:

> *David's son Absalom had a beautiful sister named Tamar, and David's son Amnon loved her. He was in such straits over his sister Tamar that he became sick; since she was a*

virgin, Amnon thought it impossible to carry out his designs toward her. Now Amnon had a son named Jonadab, son of David's brother Shimeah, who was very clever. He asked him, 'Prince why are you so dejected morning after morning? Why not tell me?' So Amnon said to him 'I'm in love with Tamar, my brother Absalom's sister.' <u>*Then Jonadab replied, 'Lie down on your bed and pretend to be sick. When your father comes to you, say to him, 'please let my sister Tamar come and encourage me to take food. If she prepares something appetizing in my presence, for me to see, I will eat it from her hand.'*</u>

That story relates to one that is from our era. There was a man who was contacted by a friend who told him that there was this promising start-up company that was seeking to raise capital. The man was asked by the friend to buy the remaining shares which were limited and costs only $300. The man went to the bank, obtained the money and was making his way to purchase the shares when another friend met him on the way and, having learnt where the man was going, said "those things never work." The second friend discouraged him and the man went and bought fishing gear instead. A few years later those shares which would have only cost him $300 were worth Eighty Million ($80,000,000.00) – the company was Microsoft.

Dr. Myles Munroe in his book *The Principles and Power of Vision* writes that we should not be "*afraid to disassociate [ourselves] from people who aren't right for you.*"[88] He continues:

Priority requires that there are people and places that you are going to have to disassociate yourself from if you're going to make it to your dream. ...you have to disassociate yourself from people who aren't going anywhere and don't want you to go anywhere in life. The sad thing is that some people literally sacrifice their dreams and their lives because they are afraid of having conflict and disagreement with others.[89]

We should then strive to have friends that facilitate our vision. Such a friend should be willing to be there for you despite what people say. Even in the midst of homosexual accusations Oprah remained steadfast:

> *I understand why people think we're gay. There isn't a definition in our culture for this kind of bond between women. So I get why people have to label it-how can you be this close without it being sexual? How else can you explain a level of intimacy where someone always loves you, always respects you, admires you? …wants the best for you in every single situation of your life. Lifts you up. Supports you. Always! That's an incredible rare thing between even the closest of friends.*[90]

Gayle even goes a step further and says *"…I have to admit it if Oprah were a man, I would marry her."*[91]

Oprah and Gayle's friendship has truly stood the test of time. In 2006, after they went on a road trip together across the U.S in a Chevy Impala Oprah could only remark *"..if you can survive 11 days in cramped quarters with a friend and come out laughing, your friendship is the real deal. I know ours is."*[92]

Tips for Practicing O'Habit #18 – Knowing the value of a good friend:

- Always remember that people are like elevators, they will either take you up or down;

- Ask yourself "with whom am I spending most of my time?";

- Disassociate yourself from those friends that are not contributing positively to your life.

O'Habit #19: Oprah Never Misses a Meeting

Method is the very hinge of business, and there is no method without punctuality.

Richard Cecil

Oprah who has a very busy schedule is known for keeping commitments and not missing a meeting. She does this with such consistency that it is mind boggling. That makes punctuality another success habit of Oprah. If she gives her word that she'll be there, she'll be there! After all Oprah has integrity!

Sonia Alleyne in the June 2008 Black Enterprise Magazine wrote that "*in her 22 years of business, [Oprah] remembers cancelling only three meetings due to dire situations.*"[93] Oprah says that the greatest fear of canceling is that "*you're going to disappoint somebody...it's no small thing. I take it personally. That's what commitment means to me.*"[94]

This trait seems to have been cultivated from childhood and her father and anyone else who assisted in raising her should be commended for assisting in developing this successful habit. Oprah proudly states that:

> *if you would go back and look at my school records, I was one of those (with) perfect attendance. I learned the meaning of excellence in the third grade because I turned in my book report early to my teacher, Mrs. Driver, and she was so impressed with me she told all the other students. They hated me every day afterwards, but it worked wonders with the rest of the teachers....but, you know,....I am going to keep the commitment.*[95]

What does this teach us? You've got to have discipline too. Moreover keeping your word can take you places and gives you a good reputation. How many times have we cancelled a meeting when it was in fact not necessary. What message are we sending when we cancel and what does that do to our name?

Let's resolve to attend all of our meetings and to be on time unless it's a dire situation.

Tips for Practicing O'Habit #19 – Punctuality:

- Use software such as Outlook and devices such as your cell phone to remind you of your appointments;

- Always check to ensure that you do not have other commitments before you make a subsequent commitment;

- Call ahead to confirm your meeting and practice asking the other party to indicate in advance if they can not make it.

O'Habit #20: Oprah Does What She Loves

I believe that success is doing what you love to do, doing the thing that you were born to do, and being paid well to do it. Period!

Delatorro McNeal II

The master in the art of living makes little distinction between,
His work and his play,
His labor and his leisure,
His mind and his body,
His information and his recreation,
His love and his religion,
He hardly knows which is which,
He simply pursues his vision of excellence in whatever he does,
Leaving others to decide whether he is working or playing,
To him, he's always doing both.

James A. Michener

I recently read somewhere that work should involve a number of things that one really likes to do and not simply a number of tasks one does to make a living. If it's one person we know who lives by this, it is Oprah. She truly does what she loves and makes it yet another success habit of hers.

She always loved talking, even at an early age. In fact she admits:

> *I use to speak in the church all the time, and the sisters in the front row fanning themselves would say to my grandmother 'Hattie Mae, this child sure can talk!'. So if those sisters were alive today wouldn't they be shocked because I'm still talking.*[96]

From the time she was a little girl Oprah loved to talk – Now she is the number one talk-show host and has kept that title for over 20 years. And even though incessant talking is a natural trait of children, who knows what she would have been doing if her grandmother would have silenced her believing like most did back then that "*children should be seen and not heard*". Oprah perhaps could be said to be fulfilling her destiny. If she had still been reading news, perhaps she would not have been enjoying the success that she is enjoying today. You see everyone has a purpose and when you walk in your purpose and you line up with your destiny, then its smooth sailing. Delatorro McNeal II echoes this "*when you do what you were born to do, there is a flow in your life. Go with that flow, not against it.*" Oprah believes that:

> *Fulfilling your purpose, with meaning, is what gives you that electrifying "juice" and makes people stand in wonder at how you do it. The secret is alignment: when you know for sure that you're on course and doing exactly what you're supposed to be doing, fulfilling your soul's intention, your heart's desire, … When your life is on course with its purpose,*

*you are your most powerful. And you may stumble but you
will not fall.*[97]

As a result of that belief, Oprah aligned herself with activities
that facilitated her gift of talking because that was something
she loved to do. We can certainly understand her image of
"electrifying juice" because we see it bursting out of her often on
her TV show.

For this very reason I encourage parents to observe the talents
and desires of their children. Do they like to paint, write, sing
or dance? Support them by buying paint brushes, karaoke set
or sending them to music lessons. They may very well be the
next John Grisham, Whitney Houston or Picasso. We oftentimes
stifle our children's creativity when we say to them "you talk too
much", or "all you are good for is writing songs". Encourage
them while teaching them to create balance by not neglecting
their school work.

My friend Sheron has a son who loves cricket and I mean
LOVES cricket. He walks, talks and dreams of cricket. Every
opportunity he gets he is with a cricket bat and a ball. My wife
teaches him at the local high school and she says that whenever the
class is given a composition to write and the topic is not dictated,
he writes about cricket. He has been doing well and I will not be
surprised if he becomes Montserrat's next greatest cricketer.

Doing what you love not only benefits the individual, but
it also benefits the wider society. Delatorro McNeal II is also
convinced of that. In his book <u>Caught Between a Dream and
a Job: How to Leave the 9-to-5 and Step Into the Life You've
Always Wanted</u> (a book that is in my opinion the best book on
the subject and a must read for everyone) he writes:

I am convinced that when we become a nation and a world full of people who do what they were born to do, and flow exclusively in that, we will have much better, cleaner, healthier neighborhoods and communities; stronger and more connected families; and thriving marriages and relationships. However, as long as most people continue to trade their time for a paycheck that they have already outgrown, in a job that they dislike and that dwarfs their potential and imprisons their purpose, we will continue to see a decline in the nucleus and fabric of our society[98].

Oprah not only does what she loves, she too encourages us to do the same. In fact, she made it a cover feature in the September 2007 issue of the Oprah Magazine. The issue featured a few women who ditched their 9-to-5 to dedicating themselves to what they love. One such person was Mary South, a publishing executive who *"pulled up anchor on her career and her life as she knew it"*, she sold her house and bought a 40-foot 30 ton steel trawler. What made it scarier was that South had no idea as to how to appreciate it. After several weeks of classes, she daringly made her first journey up the Atlantic coast from Florida to Maine. The result…well, she shares that:

The happiness I found at sea, the sense of accomplishment I felt, made it clear that I was more myself, more me, standing at the helm of my little ship that I had ever been sitting in a conference room. …I can honestly say however, that buying the Bossanova was the smartest thing I ever did. In the end, my adventure thrilled me in a way that a fat paycheck and job security never could.[99]

We should not allow looming deadlines and the desire to make more money stand in the way of our peace of mind. The greatest satisfaction we'll ever get in life will only come when we dare, like Mary and Oprah to do what we love. I end by encouraging you to do what you love and you will always be rewarded. I want to leave you with some questions of Mark Twain that resonated in my heart when I first read it and continues to resonate today:

What work I have done I have done because it has been play. If it had been work I shouldn't have done it. Who was it who said, "Blessed is the man who has found his work"? Whoever it was had the right idea in his mind. Mark you, he says his work – not somebody else's work. The work that is really a man's own work is play and not work at all. Cursed is the man who has found some other man's work and cannot lose it. When we talk about the great workers of the world, we really mean the great players of the world.[100]

Tips for Practicing O'Habit #20 – Doing what you love:

- Buy the book <u>Caught Between a Dream and a Job: How to Leave the 9-to-5 and Step Into the Life You've Always Wanted</u> . This would help you to transition from where you are to where you want to go;

- Write your plan down and begin implementing it;

- Give yourself a time limit and talk to those who are doing what you would love to do and make them a mentor.

O'Habit #21: Oprah is Real

Any emotion, if it is sincere, is involuntary.

Mark Twain

In medieval times people were great lovers of statues and traded them freely. As a trader you knew that a hairline crack in your statue could render your statue valueless. Cracks were concealed using wax. If you were buying a statue, you would ask the vendor to bring it out into the sun and let it sit there for hours so that it would melt the wax exposing the flaws of the statue. Therein lies the origin of the word "sincere" i.e "sine" which means "without" and "cera" which means "wax". That is Oprah! She is as real and sincere as they come. She must have inspired Jennifer Lopez's "*I'm real*" song. In her July 2007 "What I Know For Sure" column, she recalls many years ago when she was first sent to Hollywood as a reporter to cover ABC's new season and interview the "stars". Even though she was twenty-four and had interviewed several persons over the previous seven years, Oprah knew that interviewing celebrities was different and that her "*only saving grace lay in finding a way to be real*".[101] Even though we perceive that celebrities are superb beings who probably do not experience things like flatulence, we love Oprah because we can relate to someone who openly admits her flaws and discloses her skeletons. In a 1986 television interview Oprah told Mike Wallace:

> *The reason I communicate with these people is because I think I'm every woman and I've had every malady and I've been on every diet and I've had men who have done me wrong, honey. So I related to all that. And I'm not afraid or ashamed to say it.*[102]

For viewers then, Oprah is not some picture perfect woman with dreams and hopes that are unreachable. She is someone who shares similar set-backs, disappointments and trials. For the viewers, she is for real!

Not only is she real, but Oprah does all she can to experience what ordinary people go through. Sometimes she takes it to the extreme. In 2004, she came up with the idea of going back in time. This idea took her and Gayle on a cross country flight to the tip of Maine followed by a four hour drive to "The colony". This was truly a primitive experience in that there were no phones, no make-up, no toilet paper and no panties. While Oprah was happy to "*rough it out*", her friend Gayle was not as thrilled as she declared "*I'm a room service girl*". While there she fed pigs, had to hear mice running during the night and made breakfast without the assistance of a microwave oven. The interesting thing was she had fun with it, remembering how she unlike Gayle grew up having to feed pigs and do chores. This also showed us how human this billionaire is and makes her even more likeable.

In the early years Oprah showed up at an Oprah Show viewer's house to give them the night off while she babysat. Half way through the night the real Oprah asked "*how am I suppose to know when the pamper needs changing?"* A question that most would have asked themselves and not allow viewers to know their limitation.

Being real and being your true self is very important. Oftentimes, we tend to want to be what others want us to be and by the time we adapt to their liking, they change their minds about who they think we should be. Approval addiction is so prevalent that Joyce Myer wrote a book on the subject stating:

> *Not everyone is going to like us. I recently read somewhere that statistically 2 percent of the population won't like us, and there is nothing we can do about it but accept it and go on about our business. If we live our lives worrying about what other people think, we will never take risks or stretch ourselves into new realms. We will give up our dreams*[103].

Let's strive like Oprah to be real. Let us buy a car because we want to and not because we think others may be fond of it. In 2006, after spending two years on the island of Antigua, I returned home with my law practice and bought a Toyota Rav 4 that dated back to about 1995 or thereabout. It had no power windows a color that turned people off and was far from the ideal ride consistent with the image of an entertainment attorney. *"A man of your caliber should be driving a Mercedes or a BMW"* I was constantly told, but I was happy! The vehicle was fully paid for and I resolved that I would keep my priorities well in check. Many persons on Montserrat were (and some are still) driving nice cars while being slaves to the banks and lending institutions. I did not want to be numbered in that category. I refused to let someone else's idea determine my expenditure pattern.

It may not be easy but it takes practice. The temptation to be anything but real may stem from perhaps a desire to be accepted.

However, I dare say that we are more respected when we are real. Oprah does not endorse a movie or book unless she genuinely loves it. In showbiz, that's hard because most shows are based on ratings which are a result of popular view. Oprah however follows her gut and remains true to herself whether she's liked or not. The result – a number one television show for over twenty years. Which other talk show host comes on TV in a bath robe and without any make-up? Let us like Oprah be real and the world would be a better place.

Tips for Practicing O'Habit #21 – Being Real:

- Be true to yourself;

- If you are only doing it, saying or eating it just to please someone else then don't;

- Before you make any major purchase ask yourself "*am I really in need of this or am I only keeping up appearances?*".

O'Habit #22: Oprah is Grateful

How sharper than a serpent's tooth it is to have a thankless child.

William Shakespeare's King Lear Act I, Sc. 4

Nothing more detestable does the earth produce than an ungrateful man.

Decimus Magnus Ausonius

It is necessary to cultivate the habit of being grateful for every good thing that comes to you – to give thanks continuously.

Wallace D. Wattles

In his book "The Science of being Rich" Wallace D. Wattles writes that "*many people who order their lives rightly in all other ways are kept in poverty by their lack of gratitude.*" Oprah does not suffer from such lack. She is constantly expressing her gratitude to her staff, her partner and her friends. In fact she starts her day being grateful:

I wake up every morning rejoicing that I'm still here with an opportunity to begin again and be better. I awaken to a morning prayer of thanks posted on my bathroom wall from Marianne Williamson's book Illuminata.[104]

What better way to start your day than by acknowledging all of the things you should be happy about. This in itself sets the tone for the rest of your day –and makes your day enjoyable.

In the January 2003 issue of the Oprah Magazine she commenced her editorial column "Here We Go" by declaring that she's *"offering gratitude for health I've been granted and giving thanks that I am one year closer to an exciting new chapter in my life –the 50's"*.[105] In bringing the same year to a close she writes in the same column:

> *This holiday, give thanks for the things you absolutely wouldn't change about your life. Then take your gratitude a step further and, instead of just giving another fruit basket, offer the gift of graciousness to another.*[106]

Not only is she always finding some way to express this important virtue, she encourages others publicly to be grateful in true Oprah fashion. In bringing her 19th season to a climax she threw a party with a Hawaiian theme for the staff at Harpo. This not only exemplified the O'Habit of treating her staff well, it also said "thank you" for the countless hours of work and their dedication.

When Chicago entertainment lawyer Jeff Jacobs advised her to develop her brand, set-up her own studio, own and license the show, she rewarded him with 5% shares in her corporation. Today he owns 10% of Harpo Inc. as evidence of Oprah's gratitude to him for putting her on the right path in the business of entertainment.

Another act that demonstrated how grateful she is was her Legends Ball which featured 200 waiters, 362 guests and 6 carat diamond teardrop chandeliers as gifts – and all in the name of being grateful to *"women who had been a bridge to now in my life and how much they meant to me…"*. Marcia Z. Nelson also observes

Oprah's gratitude whereby Oprah "*invariably thanks each guest for his or her appearance and always closes the show with her thanks.*"[107]

It's a topic she herself has covered several times on her show. Oprah motivates viewers to start a Gratitude Journal – something she herself has been doing for several years. Nelson notes that :

> *Psychologists Robert A. Emmons of the University of California and Michael Mc Cullough of the University of Miami have shown that people who keep gratitude journals are healthier, more optimistic, and more satisfied with their lives than those whose journals record neutral or problematic events. They have also found that people with gratitude lists are more likely to have progressed toward an important personal goal.*[108]

The act of constantly giving thanks and showing appreciation, therefore, has health benefits and should be encouraged. Gratitude is an O'Habit that has certainly contributed to Oprah's success for, as Wattles writes, "*without gratitude you cannot keep from being dissatisfied with things as they are.*"

Tips for Practicing O'Habit #22 – Gratitude:

- Take a moment to say thank you to your spouse, girlfriend or boyfriend - be spontaneous about it;

- I agree with Mike Murdock who suggests that we should take time out and make a thanksgiving list of all the persons who you are most thankful for in your life and think of ways to express your gratitude to them;

- Practice saying thank-you for every little favor or kind gesture done for you. The use of little thank you notes is also recommended.

O'Habit #23: Oprah Forgives

Let all bitterness, wrath, and anger, and clamour, and evil speaking, be put away from you, with all malice; and be kind to one another, tenderhearted, forgiving one another, even as God for Christ's sake hath forgiven you.

Ephesians 4:31-32

For someone who has been abused and mistreated by friends, relatives and strangers, Oprah surely knows how to forgive. She has made it her business to publicly declare that she has let go of past hurtful and abusive encounters. She's known to have invited relatives on her show whom she had refused to talk to and forgive for years. That surely makes forgiveness another success habit of Oprah and certainly qualifies her to speak about it. Forgiveness is an essential trait that Oprah has adopted and that we should in turn follow. It is so much easier to hold on to the dirt that has been dished to us from childhood or past experiences. However, as John Mason has said "[I]f you quit nursing a grudge, it would die".[109]

Many fail to realize that unforgiveness blocks blessings. Recently the Warren Cassell Show did a show on forgiveness with my main guest being Rommel Lawrence, an evangelist from the island of

Dominica but based in Barbados. Lawrence recounted how he was asked to pray for a man at the Queen Elizabeth hospital. During the prayer session Lawrence noted an uneasiness in his spirit and said he was prompted by the Holy Spirit to ask the patient to rid his heart of all unforgiveness. "I have forgiven everyone" the man declared and Lawrence resumed praying but he was prompted by the Holy Spirit once again who revealed to him that the man he was praying for was sodomized at the age of 9 by a man that he had not yet forgiven. According to Lawrence, he told the man what was revealed to him and the man began crying like a child for he knew that flesh and blood could not have revealed this to Lawrence. He forgave his offender and after praying for him again, he was released from the Hospital in a few days and was no longer required to undergo the life threatening operation he was awaiting. He was miraculously healed. His healing came when he decided to forgive someone for doing something horrible to him several years ago.

What illnesses are we harboring by refusing to forgive those who hurt us? What major deal, promotion or accomplishment are we denying ourselves by unforgiveness? Brian Tracy says that:

> *The ability to forgive frees you from the past and makes you a completely different person. Virtually all negative emotions, anger, frustration, guilt, resentment, envy, jealousy, and blame arise from the inability to forgive a person for something that has been done or said in the past.*[110]

There seems to also be physiological consequences to harboring unforgiveness. Dr. Phil says that

> *When you harbor hatred, anger and resentment, your body's chemical balance is dramatically disrupted. Your 'fight-or-flight' responses stay aroused twenty-four hours a day, seven*

*days a week. That means that hatred, anger and resentment are
absolutely incompatible with your peace, joy, and relaxation.*[111]

Oprah and her producers help get that message out by
producing shows like the April 22, 2002 show "Incredible Stories
of Forgiveness", the November 15, 2000 show "How to Forgive
Yourself" and the July 25, 1996 show "I am Sorry Day". And
while she's been accused of "*preaching*", such shows are consistent
with Marcia Nelson's belief that "*showing is better than telling*".[112]

Like Oprah let us resolve to forgive those who have hurt us.
We cannot change the fact that others have hurt us but we can
surely determine how we react to the pain. Let us let go of the
past. I do not believe that Oprah could have achieved half the
success that she enjoys if she had refused to forgive her abusers,
and herself for the mistakes she's made.

Tips for Practicing O'Habit #23 – Forgiveness:

- Call the people who have really hurt you and who you
  have not forgiven to tell them you forgive them. If it's
  easier to send them flowers, do so;

- Resolve not to remind those who have hurt you of the hurt
  they caused you after you have forgiven them. You have not
  truly forgiven if you keep reminding them of the hurt;

- Examine your conscience and bring to mind those
  persons whom you have caused great pain. Call them to
  tell them that you are sorry or send them flowers and ask
  them to forgive you;

- John Mason says "*One of the secrets of a long and fruitful
  life is to forgive everybody everything every night before you
  go to bed.*" Resolve to do this each night.

O'Habit #24: Oprah Practices Humility

A person can achieve everything by being simple and humble.

Rig Vega

He who is humble is confident and wise. He who brags is insecure and lacking.

Lisa Edmondson

As an old song goes "*it's hard to be humble, when you're perfect in every way*". This is especially so in the entertainment industry. Even Oprah was forced to admit once that "*everyone has an ego*". In the entertainment industry, especially in music - in particular Hip Hop, humility is a foreign trait. In their music they boast about their possessions, women and success. Take Will Smith's "Freakin it" for example:

On the corner with your friends
Heard you screamin about cream in your rap kid
Yo my last check for wild wild west came on a flat bed
Once and for all let's get this straight
How you measure a rapper what make an mc great?

Is it the sales? - 20 mill
Is it the cars?- Bentlys
Is it the women?- Jada
Is it the money? - please
Mr. clean yet the fact remains
I Got girls that don't speak english screamin my name.[113]

A "humble" person serves; a "humble" person is teachable and a "humble" person never forgets where he or she comes from. Having regard to her success, fame and fortune, it's amazing how Oprah remains grounded and practices humility. Despite her achievements, she does not boast or in any way suggest that she is solely responsible for her success. In fact, in her commemorative DVD box set celebrating 20 years on TV she said:

I don't come to any of this without an acknowledgement of where I come from and I know that is not a small thing to be a former colored girl, negro, black, now African American in the United States with a media forum that is in the homes of millions of people in the United States and throughout the world. I did not take that lightly and to this day I do not take that lightly[114].

She's obviously grateful to God for her success and is very much honored to have been the one divinely selected for this earthly task. Oprah is also appreciative of the fact that many have received her with warm, open arms.

Oprah took humility to another level when she removed her talk show from Emmy consideration in 1999. Even though she had already won forty Emmys, removing herself was obviously a noble move and ensured that other talk show hosts were able to bask in the joy of winning an Emmy. I can hardly think of another celebrity who's willing to do that.

"*Everybody has an ego*" says Oprah, but she sure keeps hers in check. When corporate execs proposed that a new cosmetic line be launched using her name and face, Oprah turned it down even though it would have featured her likeness on signage in every major department store, included 80,000 employees nationwide and generated millions in revenue.

It's not something that is easy to do, and neither is it common especially when you are a celebrity, but practicing humility is something that we should strive to do. Oprah serves, she is teachable and never forgets where she comes from. For that we can safely say she is humble and practices humility.

Tips for Practicing O'Habit #24 – Practicing humility:

- Know your limitations and appreciate them;

- Remain teachable;

- Give God the Glory for every achievement in your life;

- Recognize that where you are today is a result of several persons' efforts including your parents, teachers and even your enemies.

O'Habit #25: Oprah Diversifies

Variety is the spice of life that gives it all its flavor
William Cowper

I believe it was Andrew Carnegie who once said "*Put your eggs in one* basket…". That can be dangerous as seen when there was an intense credit crunch and persons were being laid off from work in droves, resulting in several homes being repossessed.

Putting all of one's eggs in a single basket is certainly a philosophy that Oprah does not adhere to and it's not by chance, it is very much on purpose. Several years ago she told Forbes, "*On my own I will just create, and if it works it works, and if it doesn't, I'll create something else. I don't have any limitations now on what I think I could do or be.*"[115] That's exactly what she has set out to do. When she was peaking in the late eighties no one had a magazine, a radio broadcast or television network in mind, yet several years later she added different arms to her media empire to encompass those media tentacles. In addition to the Oprah Winfrey show, there is Harpo Print LLC which supervises the partnership between Hearst (Publisher of the Oprah Magazine) and Harpo Inc., Harpo Radio Inc. which handles the "Oprah

& Friends" broadcast through XM Satellite radio, Harpo Films which produces approximately two feature films per year, Oprah. com which reaches 5 million unique users per month, she has more recently acquired the Oprah Winfrey Network. All these are housed in several buildings in the heart of Chicago known to some as "the campus".

Tim Bennett, president of Harpo Inc. says that:

> *the goal for the company is to have enough legs on the table that if you take away 'The Oprah Winfrey Show' which is supposed to go till 2011, the table doesn't fall over and we'll have enough other businesses to keep us active and keep Oprah's platform in the world.*[116]

That's the reason why mutual funds are so successful. Rather than investing your money in one particular commodity or service, your monies are invested in a plethora of various commodities so that the investment is less risky.

In 2008, Oprah told Black Enterprise magazine's Sonia Alleyne that over the past 15 years, she's been repeatedly telling her team that the talk show was "*just the beginning.*" Now several years later, she's taken Harpo Inc. from being a five person company to a 500 employee multimedia conglomerate – by not placing all her eggs in one basket. Let's master this O'Habit and learn to diversify.

Tips for Practicing O'Habit #25 – Diversifying:

- Find ways of generating income other than by what you are currently doing. This does not mean changing your career, but finding other revenue streams that compliment it. For example, you may be a plumber that has been in the business for over twenty years. You have twenty years experience that you can draw from to write a book or create a website dealing with common plumbing problems and solutions;

- Examine your talents outside your profession and brainstorm as to how you can generate income from them.

O'Habit #26: Oprah Exercises Daily

Do not worry, eat three square meals a day, say your prayers, be courteous to your creditors, keep your digestion good, exercise, go slow and easy.

Abraham Lincoln (1809 -1865)

Working out slows the aging process and makes you more vital. Aha! Aha! Aha!

Oprah Winfrey

Although she has the best support staff, and the funding to keep the show at number one for twenty years, Oprah could not have done it in bad health. No matter what ideas we have, we could only effectively implement them if we are healthy. And there's no shortcut to being healthy. On turning fifty she said *"If there were a shortcut to having a healthy body, I'm sure I'd have the secret by now."*[117] In drafting the outline for this book, I had a chapter titled "Oprah Treats Her Body Well". As I was about to write this chapter, I realized that the title was indeed broad and it was necessary to particularize the habits that would make one conclude Oprah does in fact treat her body well. I found three –

exercising, eating well and resting. These are consistent with what Oprah says about one's body in the June 2006 issue of the Oprah magazine: "*You must nurture it, work it, rest it.*" The next three O-habits are therefore about treating your body well and we will indeed start with exercising.

We live in a world of luxury - we drive to work, we work in air conditioning and getting up to change the channel is no longer a complaint thanks to the remote control. If we as ordinary folks enjoy these everyday comforts, just imagine Oprah! She lives a pampered life that allows for very little physical activity. Exercising is therefore compulsory in order for her to keep fit and healthy.

The more physical our daily work, the less need for exercise. I was recently speaking to a friend who told me that his mother and grandmother ate more butter and fat than we do; they used much more salt than we do and even consumed more alcohol than we do, yet they didn't die from any degenerative diseases. The reason for this he believed was because his grandmother got up in the morning and had to walk maybe five miles to plough farmland, plant fruits and vegetables in the hot sun only to return home at the end of the day after another five mile journey.

Rather than using a washing machine, they had to find a river and wash their clothes. They rode a donkey or walked to work. In addition they had to keep up with their briskly-walking sheep, goats and other animals when tethering them daily. Their exercise regimen was already wrapped up in their daily activity. They didn't need any tread mill, ab machine or stairmaster. Moreover, there were no vehicles to take them to work – not that I am knocking these luxuries for as Stormie Omartian says in her book "Greater health God's Way: 7 steps to inner and outer Beauty", "...*there is nothing in the world wrong with using modern conveniences if you are replacing the physical labor you've lost with some form of exercise.*"[118]

Oprah knows the benefit of exercise and makes it a part of her daily routine. She believes that:

When you nurture and support your body, it reciprocates. The basis of that support is exercise, like it or not. The most essential benefit is more energy. The bonus is weight control.[119]

As such she employed a personal trainer over 15 years ago and has been exercising daily. She knows exercising helps maintain a healthy weight, slows down aging and increases circulation. Stormie Omartian sums it up well when she writes:

When you are engaged in any form of exercise you breathe deeply and inhale more oxygen. This oxygen enters the bloodstream through tiny blood vessels in the lungs. The heart pumps more blood, which carries this oxygen to the rest of the body. Toxins and waste products in the form of carbon dioxide are removed from the bloodstream at that time and expelled back through the lungs during exhalation. The more oxygen in your body, the purer the bloodstream.... When the blood is clean, disease cannot breed there.[120]

So important is exercise to Oprah that she built a gym at work so that her staff too can develop and maintain this healthy habit. When she first started she was not allowed to have a treadmill in the office and when she left the network and got her own show, building and equipment, she outfitted it with a gym and spa. Now, she gets up and arrives at work around 6:00 am, exercises, showers and heads straight to her make-up room. Exercise should not be done only when one feels like it, but rather it should be incorporated into your daily life. It surely is for Oprah. Despite the money she has made and all of her achievements, she still maintains that "*Taking care of your body, no matter what your age, is an investment. The return is priceless.*"[121]

Tips for Practicing O'Habit #26 – Exercising:

- Allocate at least 5 days per week for exercising. It would be easier to find someone to work out with you so that you have encouragement. This also will make it more likely to be consistent;

- Vary the Exercises. Perhaps weights one day and cardio another;

- Purchase Tae Bo or other exercise DVDs and use them to help vary the walking or running you plan to do;

- Park your car far from the supermarket so you get a good walk bearing in mind that the physical activity will be beneficial to you;

- Be consistent! And burn the candle at both ends by eating healthily. Your results will double.

O'Habit #27: Oprah Eats Healthily

The King who cannot rule his diet, will hardly rule his realm in peace and quiet.

**Passage from the "Rule of health of Salerno",
author unknown**

If you don't take care of yourself, the undertaker will overtake that responsibility for you.

Carrie Latet

Your body is a necessary tool to fulfill your purpose on earth and you should be careful what you consume. Stormie Omartian writes:

> *You must make up your mind to have respect, love and appreciation for the body God gave you, no matter what shape it is in at this moment. ...I don't care how much money Aunt Mildred left you or how good your health insurance is, you cannot afford to be sick. Sickness detracts from our relationships and service far more than we can imagine. God designed the body to be self-repairing and self healing if we treat it properly.*[122]

In order to maintain a healthy body, Oprah adopts the habit of eating healthily.

We already know that physical exercise is an excellent way to keep the body healthy. However, exercising daily while eating junk or even eating emotionally would negate all exercise efforts. Oprah concurs by admitting *"the resolve to work out is directly tied to eating healthfully."* Having eaten her way through depression and battling with her weight in her earlier years she has matured and declares that *"events that used to leave me reeling, with my head in a bag of chips, no longer faze me."*

Unfortunately, eating properly tends to be hard and we normally get the impetus to eat properly when we put on a little weight. For some, eating properly is what we call diets and as far as those are concerned, Oprah admits that she's *"fallen prey to every diet scam known to womankind."* That was prior to meeting Bob Green of course, her personal trainer. Now, Oprah knows the value of eating well. She knows that:

> *You can't eat junk and expect to have an unjunked life. It's true that you are what you eat, what you think, what you believe, what you do. Eating well, making healthy choices, delicious choices, enticing choices is symbolic of how you treat yourself, and it shows. Your skin, your hair, your eyes, your energy level, your attitude, are all affected by what you ingest.* [123]

It doesn't mean that you can't have a little chocolate now and then. We should try to make each meal a pleasure *"even if it's something as simple as a crisp apple with thin slices of Parmesan, it should be delicious and aesthetically satisfying."* [124]

Tips for Practicing O'Habit #27 – Eating healthily:

- Increase your fruit and vegetable consumption;

- Drink lots of water;

- Supplement your diet with vitamin supplements. Symmetry line of vitamins is one of the best if not the best. Their fruit and vegetable based products are in no way synthetic;

- Limit your sugar consumption and avoid sodas and other carbonated beverages;

- Avoid refined foods.

O'Habit #28: Oprah Surrounds herself with positive friends

The key is to keep company only with people who uplift you, whose presence calls forth your best.

Epictetus – Greek Philosopher

Bad company corrupts good morals.

1 Cor. 15:33

We have all heard the adage "*you are known by the company you keep.*" Keeping good company or surrounding herself with positive friends is yet another O'Habit. Gayle, her BFF, is as Oprah says "*one of the nicest persons on earth*" and the two seem inseparable. Maya Angelou who acts more like a mother figure has been a spiritual pillar for her. Virtually all her associates help keep Oprah stable and grounded for after all, as the saying goes "*people are like elevators, they either take you up or down*".

In a show on Authentic Power, author Gary Zukav said it well when he told Oprah that we should examine our relationships:

So look around you and see who are the people that surround you. Are they angry? Are they jealous? That's a reflection of your orientation. Is your world filled with loving caring people? Then that is reflecting your orientation and that will not change the orientation until you change[125].

Not only does Oprah employ this habit in her personal life, she does it professionally as well. She is known for keeping positive associates to the point where it affects her Radio and TV show content. Take for example her empire and how she developed "Oprah and Friends" on her satellite radio programme. Nate Berkus, Laura Berman and Gayle King form part of a cadre of positive people who uplift the spirits of listeners and contribute to a better standard of living. No longer are Oprah and her views the center of content for the shows, she wants to share her friends' views as well. Whether its interior designing, relationships or finances, its hard to dispute that it is the associates of Oprah that have contributed to the show's success. Both the radio show and the TV show cannot be said to be about Oprah alone even though she is the nucleus.

We have already seen in O-Habit #18 the destructive force of a negative friend. Dr. Myles Munroe echoes:

The law of association states that you become like those with whom you spend time. We often underestimate other's influence in our lives. There are two words that most accurately describe influence: powerful and subtle. Often you don't know you're being influenced until it is too late. Whether you realize it or not, however, the influence of those you spend time with has a powerful effect on how you will end up in life, on whether you will succeed or fail.[126]

Just like the accounting system the law of association is a double entry system. If we are to in fact associate ourselves with positive friends it would also mean that we disassociate ourselves from negative influences. Dr. Munroe encourages that we should not "*be afraid to disassociate ourselves from people who aren't right for you.*"[127] He says that "*priority requires that there are people and places that you are going to have to disassociate yourself from if you're going to make it to your dream.*"[128]

You should be encouraged to tell the boyfriend or girlfriend who is keeping you from achieving your dreams to hit the road, especially if you know deep down that that relationship is preventing you from fulfilling your purpose.

The relationships we form would in fact determine the path our life will take. It is therefore important to, like Oprah, surround ourselves with positive friends.

Tips for Practicing O'Habit #28 – Surrounding yourself with positive friends:

- Form positive long lasting relationships;

- Disassociate yourself from persons who look more like your destruction rather than your destiny;

- Do all you can to ensure that you are a positive influence on your friends.

O'Habit #29: Oprah Listens

A friend is someone who helps you up when you're down, and if they can't, they lay down beside you and listen.

Unknown

No one is as deaf as the man who will not listen.

Jewish Proverb

One of the reasons why Oprah dominates the talk-show circuit is because she is a good listener. In any given interview she spends more than half the time listening to her guest. Why? Because as Marcia Z. Nelson says *"Listening has power. It is a mark of respect and acknowledges someone's existence and experience."*[129] Oprah knows that everyone wants to be validated and in receiving the Bob Hope Humanitarian Award at the 2002 Prime Time Emmy Awards said:

> *The greatest pain in Life is to be invisible....what I've learned is that we all just want to be heard. And I thank all the people who continue to let me hear your stories, and by sharing your stories, you let other people see themselves and, for a moment, glimpse the power to change and the power to triumph.*

Listening then is an important habit that has contributed to her success. It's almost as if she's a professional shrink and most flock to her show to sit on her couch and spill their guts for Oprah to listen. In fact I am amazed at the things people freely say to Oprah and millions of viewers when they are otherwise afraid to even tell their spouse. For example, Mackenzie Phillips in the Fall of 2009 told Oprah how she had sexual intercourse with her father. Not only did listening to her guest help to ease the pain the guest endured, it also allowed other people to come forward seeking to have Oprah listen to their story as well.

Larry King who I think is the King of talk says:

To be a good talker, you must be a good listener. This is more than just a matter of showing an interest in your conversation partner. Careful listening makes you better able to respond – to be a good talker when it's your turn. Good follow-up questions are the mark of a good conversationalist.[130]

How many times have you heard your spouse or partner say *"You're not listening to me!"*?. I've personally lost count and am resolving to be a better listener. Listening as a talk-show host is good but as an individual at home, as a student in class or as an employee we ought to listen more. Too often we concentrate on speaking abilities and fail to stress the importance of listening. Have you ever met someone who talks so much that you are not able to get a word in? There's a gentleman I know like this and every time I see him I sigh. Having a conversation with him only allows me to say "good morning" and he takes over. I am hardly able to get a word in. It's a sign of being self absorbed and Oprah surely displays that she is selfless.

Adopting the habit of listening can only improve our communication skills, bearing in mind that communication is a two-way street. Let's therefore resolve to listen.

Tips for Practicing O'Habit #29 – Listening

- Practice listening to what the other person is saying to you before answering or commenting;

- Do not cut the other person off even if you know what they are saying;

- Repeat sometimes the instruction or the concern of the other person to confirm that you are both on the same page.

O'Habit #30: Oprah Values Time

Time is a seed, and the manner in which you spend your time will determine the harvest you will reap.

Ivenia Benjamin

Time is the coin of your life. It is the only coin you have, and only you can determine how it will be spent. Be careful lest you let other people spend it for you.

Carl Sunburg

Time consciousness is very important to Oprah who after turning fifty wrote "*I am more aware of time now than I have ever been before.*"[131] This consciousness seems to have developed over time and demonstrates that she has definitely become wiser having attained the age of fifty. Moreover, her newly awoken awareness of time is also consistent with her "*live your best life*"[132] motto.

Given Oprah's fame and success, she is perhaps forced to be time conscious. Phones are constantly ringing, several emails are being sent to her and numerous requests are made for her appearance on magazine covers and special events. Oprah's time is so precious that every minute of her day is accounted for.

She has no regrets about her busy life, once proclaiming "*My schedule is very hectic, but it's exactly the kind of life I've always wanted. I've always wanted to be so busy that I wouldn't have time to breathe.*"[133] She has a plethora of assistants that screen her calls to ensure that time wasters do not waste her precious time. When you enter the homes of millions of people daily via the medium of television, viewers become attached to you and somehow feel that you are their personal friend. Over the years Oprah has had to carefully select the people she meets or with whom she speaks. In fact, she once told Time magazine that she used:

> ...*to take every phone call from a guy who said he would jump off a building if I didn't talk to him. But I no longer feel compelled to aid every crazy. For two years I have done everything everyone asked me to do. I am now officially exhausted.*[134]

Like Oprah we need to resolve to make sure we make the best of our time. In addition, Mike Murdock enlightens us further saying that "a *major difference exists between the poor and the powerful; the pauper and the prosperous. That difference is the management of time.*"[135]

And how exactly do we manage our time? Oprah says that she's "*working on not letting people with dark energy consume any of my time.*"[136] I recall how I implemented a consultation fee at my office. I was drafting a claim in the High Court and was constantly being interrupted by clients who by the end of speaking to them for 30 minutes, I had to advise that there was no legal basis for a claim. As a result, by the end of the month I would have spent hours listening to them, analyzing their situations and advising them while receiving no fees. At the end of one long drawn out meeting an elderly lady left my office and said thank you. While that was appreciated, I immediately instructed my assistant to place a notice in the front office that a consultation fee of $100 for a half hour consultation is to be paid prior to speaking with me. In this way my time is not wasted. In the United States, most lawyers charge a fee every time you contact them by phone.

Time lost can never be regained and Oprah believes that "*how you spend your time defines who you are.*" Ivenia Benjamin concurs with this when she writes:

> *Whatever you spend your time pursuing, that thing will increase in your life. If you spent your time and money in a bar buying and drinking alcohol every night, you are planting a seed of alcoholism and before long you will be an addicted alcoholic. Whatever you give yourself to will also take over your life. If you spend your time in prayer you will reap the benefits of a life of prayer.*[137]

Let's resolve like Oprah to value our time. I've promised myself that I would dedicate quality time to my dreams and the visions God has given to me. While writing this book, I have had to decline many offers to attend parties and beach gatherings. In fact, my exact words to my friend Victor when invited to go to the beach was "*sorry, I've got to finish my 'best seller'.*"

Time is one of God's greatest gifts and is to be valued above all tangible objects and although you may gain more money from valuing your time, Oprah cautions us that "*…all the money in the world doesn't mean a thing if you don't have time to enjoy it.*"[138] Let's resolve to spend ours wisely.

Tips for Practicing O'Habit #30 – Valuing Time:

- Make purposeful appointments. Mike Murdock says that he refuses to allow anyone to walk off the streets and meet him for an appointment;

- When making appointments, set an end time. So, if the appointment is from 3pm to 3:30pm, the persons would need to be punctual so that they can maximize the time spent with you. If they are five valuable minutes late then they have thrown away five minutes of time they could have spent with you;

- No matter how busy you become, make time for your spouse and children;

- Teach others to respect your time. If you have not budgeted for it in your day, say no.

O'Habit #31: Oprah Keeps a Daily Schedule

The secret of your future is hidden in your daily routine.

Mike Murdock

There cannot be a crisis today; my schedule is already full.

Henry Kissinger

I once saw a documentary called "A Day in the life of the United States President" or something of that sort and I was amazed to learn that from about 5:30am to 10pm when he goes to bed, the United States President's time is accounted for. Whether it was eating breakfast or making a call to another leader of a first world country, the details were written down the day before and his entire day was planned. Oprah may not be the President of the United States but she sure is busy and, as the previous O'Habit explains, she values her time. Therefore, keeping a daily schedule is a must in her life.

Keeping a schedule is about planning one's day so as to make the best of that day or what you hope to accomplish tomorrow. According to Brian Tracy:

one of the most important habits you can develop is the habit
of daily goal setting. Countless people I have taught this to
have told me over the years that the power of this process is
absolutely incredible![139]

Scheduling your day is important because it promotes productivity. We tell young people that it is important to set goals in life yet we fail to see that goal setting is both macro as well as micro. Sure it is great to say you want to become a doctor, but what are you planning for tomorrow that is going to bring you closer to that goal. Successful people are people with diaries and/ or day planners. In the DVD set celebrating the 20th Anniversary of the Oprah Winfrey Show we get to see how Oprah spends her day. At one point her Chief of Staff, Libby, greets her while she is putting her make-up on and goes through her schedule for the day which included things like calling the dog breeder, going through her mails and a weekly meeting with the Executive Producer Ellen Rakieten. We see Oprah explaining:

I have four assistants. At least three or two, maybe all four
will be coming in the room giving me the schedule for the
day because most people think that the show is the thing, but
it is one of many events that happens during the day, then I
have a whole other life after the show.[140]

Planning your day also minimizes the possibility of your being distracted by time wasters. Mike Murdock illustrates:

A few days ago, someone said to me, "I want to come to
your house and spend a couple of days just knocking around
talking. When will you be home?" I laughed. What a joke!
"I don't knock around, I answered. There is not a day in my

life that I do not schedule something that matters. I keep my schedule and I am always moving toward my future.[141]

Like Oprah we need to schedule our day and write down each evening what we intend to accomplish the next day. It would at least add some purpose to living.

Tips for Practicing O'Habit #31 – Keeping a daily schedule:

- Make a schedule of things to do each night, and as you get up begin to attend to them highlighting those that are done. It's good to get a diary to keep these daily tasks in;

- Stick to your schedule unless it's something extra-ordinary;

- Let others know you have a schedule and you would not arbitrarily go beyond it.

O'Habit #32: Oprah Retreats to Rejuvenate

Come apart and rest a little….

Jesus to his disciples in Mark 6:31

W hy do you think Jesus told his disciples come apart and rest a little? Perhaps it is because if they did not rest a little, they would be no good to themselves or anyone else. Oprah too believes it is essential to not only rest, but to take it to another level and retreat in order to rejuvenate. She built a teahouse surrounded by hundreds of rose bushes, thousands of hydrangeas, and a sea of dahlias where she could go to get away from it all. "I need it to restore myself" she says.

It wasn't until she was in her twenties that she figured out how to regulate her energy. She writes:

I'd taken a job as a reporter and was working hundred hour weeks trying to be a team player. It was only after I became depleted that I realized I had only a certain amount of energy and I needed to conserve and restore it. Now when I begin to feel exhausted, I pull back. If I'm at work and people are lined up at my desk with one request after another, I literally go sit in my closet and refuel. [142]

John Mason, bestselling author of "An Enemy Called Average" also agrees with this notion and says we should in fact "retreat to advance". I practice to take at least five days out of each year on a personal retreat. No cell phones, no children and absolutely no distractions. It is in these moments ideas flow. I am rested and I become energized.

Brian Tracy says *"the greatest men and women of all ages have practiced solitude regularly. Men and women who practice it correctly and on a regular basis never fail to be amazed at the difference it makes in their lives."* [143] It would have been mentally and physically taxing for Oprah to record 2-4 shows in one day and still record promos, conduct her countless meetings and facilitate every journalist and media house seeking an exclusive. That Oprah rushes to her closet (which is much bigger than the average and is described by her as like *"shopping at Saks Fifth"*), may seem simple, but five or ten minutes in that closet puts fatigue at bay. In turn, the absence of fatigue lowers your resistance to the emotions of fear and worry.

Dale Carnegie, Author of "How to Stop Worrying and Start Living" says that *"preventing fatigue tends to prevent worry"* and encourages us to sleep for at least an hour during the day because *"an hour's nap before the evening meal plus six hours' sleep at night-a total of seven hours-will do you more good than eight hours of unbroken sleep."* [144] And what if you cannot nap for an hour? Carnegie suggests even a five to ten minute rest works wonders. No wonder Oprah retreats to her closet when she finds the need to refuel.

Despite having to record sometimes ten shows in one week and in between the hundreds of appearances, interviews and countless meetings, Oprah maintains a fresh look each appearance – and while very few people can rival the talent of her make-up artiste, Reggie Wells, I dare say that such a fresh look has little to do with make-up. Oprah sure knows the importance of retreating to rejuvenate.

Tips for Practicing O'Habit #32 – Retreating to Rejuvenate:

- Take at least seven days out of the year to relax and do nothing work related. It is suggested that you go to a secluded place and turn off your cell phone;

- Do not let your friends know where you are. Tell only one person and let him/her and your friends know how important it is to get away;

- Allow your partner/spouse time to do the same thing;

- Write your goals for the next year down and draft a plan as to how to achieve them;

- Go for long walks during this "get away" period.

O'Habit #33: Oprah Takes Sundays Off

Six days you shall labor and do all your work. But the seventh day is a sabbath to the LORD your God; you shall not do any work-you, your son or your daughter, your male or female slave, your livestock, or the alien resident in your towns. For in six days the LORD made heaven and earth, the sea, and all that is in them, but rested the seventh day; therefore the LORD blessed the sabbath day and consecrated it.

Exodus 20: 8-11

While some work 7 days per week and keep going until they die or become seriously ill, Oprah resolved years ago that she was going to make Sunday her day of rest.

Although she works hard, she sure knows that giving herself time to just be and not do is essential. How does she do this?

I give myself Sunday. Sometimes I spend the whole day in my pajamas, sometimes I have church under the trees communing with nature...most times I just do nothing-piddling, I call it-and let my brain and body decompress from six days of nonstop mental bombardment. If I didn't do that, I would implode literally, in a crazy psychic breakdown.[145]

Stormie Omartian seems to be in agreement with Oprah when she writes in her book Greater Health God's Way that the day you take off should "*be a day when you don't worry about the bills, your mind doesn't labour over your work project, you don't stop by the office, and you don't clean the house. You rest from all you do throughout the week.*"[146]

While keeping Sundays free has its genesis in the fourth of the ten commandments, taking Sundays off is also one of the best ways to improve productivity. However, the day need not be Sunday for those who must work on Sunday. What is important is that a full day is reserved to unwind and do absolutely nothing as far as work is concerned.

There is something spiritually and physically rejuvenating about keeping this day free. So important was the idea of taking this day off that to this day, it is unlawful to carry out commercial activity in South Carolina on Sundays:

On the first day of the week, commonly called Sunday, it shall be unlawful for any person to engage in worldly work, labour, business of his ordinary calling or the selling or offering to sell, publicly or by telephone, at retail or at wholesale to the consumer any goods, wares or merchandise or to employ others to engage in work, labor, business or selling or offering to sell any goods, wares or merchandise, excepting work of necessity or charity. Provided, that in Charleston County the foregoing shall not apply to any person who conscientiously believes, because of his religion, that the seventh day of the week ought to be observed as the Sabbath and who actually refrains from secular business or labor on that day.[147]

In 1912 the United States Congress passed the Mann Sunday Closing Act. This piece of legislation closed post offices on Sundays giving postal employees at least one day of rest. This law was obviously influenced by Christianity. Nowadays, stores are opened every day except Thanksgiving and Christmas.

I believe Oprah takes Sundays off because it relieves stress. She has noted the difference whenever she fails to practice this habit by admitting that *"whenever I've slipped up and missed a Sunday, I've noticed a definite change in my disposition for the rest of the week."*[148]

Like Oprah let us resolve to take a day out of the week to do nothing apart from the necessities such as bathing, cooking etc. Let us use that day to purge ourselves of any work concerns so that we can be fully energized the next day. Taking Sundays off is indeed another success habit of Oprah.

Tips for Practicing O'Habit #33 – Taking Sundays Off:

- Turn off the cell phone and refuse to do anything work related on Sunday – That includes checking email or even logging on to Facebook if you use it for networking;

- Have your children and spouse who may answer the home phone let others know that you are unavailable and would be for the duration of the day. There will be obviously times when you have an emergency;

- Go out to lunch with the family at least one Sunday per month. In that way, you avoid the task of cooking if you are the one responsible for cooking;

- Spend this time with your family since if you are busy you tend to neglect them during the week;

- Announce to your friends that the particular day is "my time" and is not to be violated;

- Ensure that you attend to any work related activity on Saturday in preparation for resting on Sunday.

O'Habit #34: Oprah learns from her Mistakes

The past should be a springboard, not a hammock.

Edmond Burke

The mistake-riddled life is much richer, more interesting, and more stimulating than the life that has never risked or taken a stand on anything.

David McNally

While it may seem that Oprah is perfect, she herself admits that she has made several mistakes in her life. However she sees those mistakes as lessons to be learnt:

Learn from your mistakes. For every crisis or mistake that comes into my life, the first question I ask is: 'what is it here to teach me?' And I ask that question because I'm looking for what is the truth in it.[149]

John Mason in his book <u>Know your Limits then Ignore Them</u> agrees with Oprah and says *"you can't travel the road to success without a puncture or two. Mistakes are often the best teachers."*[150]

Oprah then is teachable and recognizes her shortcomings and endeavors to learn not to repeat them.

One of the mistakes Oprah made which she constantly talks about is the management approach she adopted at Harpo Inc. "*I've made a lot of mistakes because I was going to run a business like a family. That doesn't work. People need management training.*" Oprah got this important lesson having moved from a staff of just a handful in the 80's to now a staff of over 700. She explains:

> *The biggest mistake in the beginning was not understanding that you need infrastructure and systems in order to run a business. And that there's a reason why there's a hierarchy in reporting systems in business. You can't handle a business like a friendship. I started out with four or five of us, and then there were eight, and then there were 22. And I kept trying to manage it as though there were still the four of us. And it wasn't until 1994 that I actually brought in someone to be President and organize the systems. I was a crazy person, trying to do it all.*[151]

She also pleads guilty of "*doing irresponsible television without even knowing it – all in the name of 'entertainment'.*" She has referred countless times to the episode during which a wife, whose husband was in an adulterous sex scandal, was made aware of the affair for the first time and before millions of viewers. Oprah shows great remorse every time she talks or writes about it. In the July 2003 issue of the Oprah Magazine she writes:

> *It's a moment I have never forgotten: The humiliation and despair on that woman's face made me ashamed of myself for putting her in that position. Right then I decided I'd never again be part of a show that demeans, embarrasses, or diminishes another human being. I replaced the 'if it bleeds,*

*it leads' news philosophy with an intention that still guides
me – to use the medium of television for its higher good.
Once the light bulb came on for me that day, my calling
became to create shows that encourage and inspire as much
as they entertain… I don't know how many years I'll be
blessed with the privilege of reaching millions each day, but
my prayer is that I'll use my energy never to belittle but to
uplift. Never to devastate but to rebuild. Never to misguide
but to light the way so that all of us can stand on higher
ground.*[152]

It is this desire to "rebuild" and "uplift" which has attracted
millions to her over the years. The lessons she has learnt have
been life changing. While at times it may seem as if Oprah is
impulsive, her actions are often propelled by lessons learnt from
previous mistakes.

Shortly after moving to Chicago in the 80's, Oprah started
a mentorship program for teenage girls living in some housing
projects. She was only able to work with them once a week
which she says "*wasn't enough time to instill values in girls whose
upbringing wasn't aligned with my teachings. I had to end the
program.*" [153] After a few months she then came up with the idea
of moving families out of the projects into their own homes. She
sums up the experience:

*I had taken for granted that they understood what it means
to go to work, be on time, and make sure their children go to
school and do their homework. So I failed with the idea, but I
learned something invaluable: In order to make the meaningful
changes, you have to transform the way people think.*[154]

She admits her failure and recognizes the valuable lesson. True transformation doesn't come from the outside but from within. Her Leadership Academy for Girls in South Africa seems to be an extension of this theory. She is directly involved in the lives of those girls. Now as she says "m*y cup runneth over as I see these girls' faces the light of my own.*"[155]

Learning from your mistakes is an O-Habit we definitely need to adopt. Ask the question Oprah asked in the May 2003 issue of the Oprah Magazine "*Will you languish in a history you can't revise or begin scripting a new experience?*"[156] I, myself have made several mistakes but like Oprah I constantly tell myself "*you've been blessed with the chance to create a new story-now take it. You've been raised. Now rise above it.*"[157]

Tips for Practicing O'Habit #34 – Learning from your mistakes:

- Do not replay painful experiences in your mind;

- Admit your mistakes and resolve to let go;

- Write down lessons you've learnt from these mistakes;

- Make reparation for mistakes you may have made in the past.

O'Habit #35: Oprah is Passionate

A strong passion for any object will insure success, for the desire of the end will point the means.

William Hazlitt

Passion is more important than brains or talent. I have seen some really talented, brainy people fail because of lack of passion.

Donald Trump

Whenever we read or hear about passion it's often in relation to a strong sexual desire - but this chapter however is not at all addressing sexual desire. It is about having an extravagant fondness, enthusiasm or desire for life and what you do in it – and that is Oprah: *"I'm a person who lives my life with great passion, and I think that comes across on the camera."*[158] For her, it's not just a word but a way of life:

Passion. I love to say the word out loud just to hear the sound of it. It resonates with me, causing me to think of all the experiences that fuel me, give me my juice: my work, speaking in front of 50 people or 5,000 and seeing someone have an aha moment, my great friendships, my dogs, the trees in my front yard, my wondrous, amazing, unfolding life.[159]

Oprah develops such a passion about her dreams and visions that it seems contagious. Often, her viewers become passionate about the same things. Take the act of giving for example. Oprah managed to cause viewers to save their spare change to deposit it in what some still call the largest public piggy bank. That gave birth to the Angel Network Foundation. Those who were not saving began gathering their loose change and hundreds were able to obtain a college degree as a result.

"Oprah's Big Give" reality show is another example where Oprah uses passion and combines it with an act which most people prefer to be on the receiving end – giving. We then began to see giving in a totally different manner. She told the 2008 graduating class at Stanford University "*If you really want to fly just harness your power to your passion.*" How badly do you want your dreams to come true? Has God given you an idea? What actions have you taken to help those dreams and ideas manifest in the earth realm? Donald Trump says that there are many people with great ideas, but they never do anything about them. In his book Think Big and Kick Ass in Business and Life he writes:

The ideas always stay in their heads and never get in their hearts. Without heart the ideas fizzle out fast. Ideas themselves are light and fluffy. They need tremendous passion to make them concrete, stone, and glass. You have to bring your ideas down to earth. Take your ideas and add the weight of passion to them as soon as possible before they disappear into thin air. Passion is the magic ingredient that zaps you with the fierce drive for completion of every endeavor. I have seen less-talented people propel themselves to great success on high-octane passion. You must have it to compete and thrive in this world.[160]

As an adult, Oprah loved the book the <u>Colour Purple</u>. She was so in love with the novel that she bought several copies and gave them out as gifts. She spoke about the book with everyone she came into contact with. She became fired up. When the opportunity arose to audition for a part in the movie she wanted to be a part. She was so passionate about it that she was not prepared to accept no for an answer. Not only did she get the part but she was nominated for an Academy award – a big deal for a first time actress. It was her relentless pursuit that got her the role. Dr. Myles Munroe asks:

> *Are you hungry for your vision? How badly do you want what you're going after? Passion is stamina that says 'I'm going to go after this, no matter what happens. If I have to wait ten years, I'm going to get it.' …if you want to go all the way to your dream, you can't sit back and expect everything to be easy. You must have purpose that produces passion.*[161]

Whether you are called to be a secretary, a doctor, a lawyer, a teacher or a domestic engineer, do like Oprah and pursue your goals, dreams and/or visions with passion. After all she says *"passion is the log that keeps the fire of purpose blazing."*[162]

Tips for Practicing O'Habit #35 – becoming passionate:

- Write down a list of things that you love to do;

- Make a list of your dreams and visions;

- Resolve to become fired up about them and pursue them relentlessly.

O'Habit #36: Oprah Follows Her Instincts

I feel there are two people inside of me – me and my intuition. If I go against her, she'll screw me everytime, and if I follow her, we get along quite nicely.

Kim Basinger

Often you have to rely on intuition.

Bill Gates

While most companies focus on revenue to justify a business decision, Oprah taps into her gut to determine whether or not it will bring revenue. She does what she calls a "gut check":

I get a lot of attention for being a businesswoman, and I have received accolades for it, but it certainly is not a strength of mine. That's not what I can do best. —the business of the business, handling the bills and making sure everybody is on point. That's draining for me. That feeling —whatever you call it: intuition, inner voice, the spirit of yourself, higher self, whatever —is how I operate in business. That's what made me

*decide that I would own my own show.... And every other
decision that I've made in my life has been based upon that
feeling – that feeling of what is the right thing to do.*[163]

Even in the earlier years when she hired staff, she relied on
"the gut check" before making the decision to hire that person.
*"I would just spend a few minutes doing my own emotional check
of how I felt about this person, whether I sensed their honesty."*[164]
Oprah believes that *"Your gut is your inner compass."*[165]

Gayle King, her best friend and XM radio host says that
"she's got a really good gut, and her gut doesn't fail her."[166] Even
if it means ignoring possible financial gain, following her gut
takes precedence in Oprah's life. One of the best examples of
Oprah letting her gut feeling supersede tremendous financial
projected revenue was several years ago when a large cosmetics
company proposed a line for women of color. The deal would
have included 80,000 employees nationwide and shelf space in
every major department store. Nonetheless, Oprah turned down
the offer all because she didn't feel it in her gut. Notwithstanding
the financial benefits and the brand recognition possibilities, she
must feel it in her gut.

On the other hand she claims that whenever she refuses
to follow her gut she regrets the decision. She refers to her
involvement with the Oxygen network as an example. Oprah
says that she went ahead with the idea because *"my lawyer at the
time and lots of other people around me said 'how are you going to
let there be a woman's network and not be a part of it?'"* Claiming
that it was *"an ego decision and not a spirited decision"* she's now
resolved to follow her gut. This explains why Oprah relinquished
all ties with Oxygen in 2007.[167]

I myself have learnt to listen to that inner voice which I
believe is the Holy Spirit. Recently, I returned from the island

of Antigua and was met by the person who had my vehicle and was responsible for cleaning it. On the way from the airport I noticed he was acting strange and seemed somewhat intoxicated. We went straight from the airport to a Quick Books class I was taking. While I was being dropped off, I clearly heard a voice telling me to have him wait for me until my class was over. I ignored the voice and asked him to return for me. He never was able to as he totaled the vehicle and was arrested an hour and a half later. I regretted not listening to that voice.

How many times have you done something you were intuitively guided not to do and did the opposite? Resolve to practice this O-habit – relying on your inner compass. As Oprah says *"when your gut is out of kilter, trouble awaits."* And *"Whenever you have to consult with other people for an answer, you're headed in the wrong direction."*[168]

Tips for Practicing O'Habit #36 – Listening to your inner compass:

- Be still, meditate and wait on your inner compass before making a decision. If you feel uncomfortable, you should decide otherwise.

O'Habit #37: Oprah Refuses To Get Flustered

Be still and know that I am God.

Psalm 46:11

It is better, I think, to grab at the stars than to sit flustered because you know you cannot reach them... At least he who reaches will get a good stretch, a good view, and perhaps even a low-hanging apple for his efforts.

R. A. Salvatore

I magine you have a job interview at 9:00am and you get up early for it. The iron has stopped working and by the time your neighbor rushes over to bring you one, you have lost your composure and you're totally flustered because you only have one chance to make a good first impression. Your neighbor calms you and you are all made up (for women) and smartly dressed (if you are a man). You jump into your car to leave only to find that the electricity just went and you're unable to leave because you've never read the manual for the new remote hydraulic gate your husband just installed. How would you react?

Worse yet - Imagine you've just landed in South Africa after travelling for eighteen (18) hours and you're unable to get off the plane because in your haste to leave the United States you forgot your passport thousands of miles away. Your initial reaction would be – PANIC!!!! Well… not Oprah, or at least not any more since she first proclaimed *"Events that used to leave me reeling, with my head in a bag of chips, no longer even faze me"*[169]. And this proclamation was made even when she forgot her passport in the U.S and only realized this when she was sitting in her jet on the tarmac in South Africa.

Oprah refuses to get flustered even if it means resorting to the child-like activity of blowing bubbles:

I keep a little bottle of bubble-blowing potion and a bubble wand on my desk. And when the day gets too heavy and I'm feeling overwhelmed, I may actually blow a few. Blowing perfect bubbles requires bringing your attention to your breath and placing it in the space of the present moment. Kind of like a bubble meditation. Being fully present automatically lifts your spirits. Clears your mind of distractions. Brings Clarity. Even some joy, if you're open to it.[170]

Catherine Ponder, one of America's foremost inspirational authors supports Oprah's habit. She writes that *"when you have a problem, if you will go into silent meditation and contemplate its solution from a divine standpoint, you will be shown what to do."*[171] I use to freak out if I was behind in a credit card payment or was being threatened to be sued. I have now learnt how to just "let go and let God" having gone through some tough times myself. I remember when I first started practicing law and was given an overdraft facility by a local bank. A few months later after things slowed down and there was little or no activity on the account (needless to say I was in overdraft) the manager called me and said that he noticed there had been no activity on my account for a while. I said to him *"What do you want me to do steal or sell my body? When the bank starts sending me work the overdraft will clear up!"* A few days later I was given substantial work and brought my payments up to date. While I may have been impertinent, I refused to stress about the bank and their concerns.

Even in these harsh economic times, Oprah advises us to remain calm. According to her in this economic state *"we have a choice: We can reside in a place of desperation, panic, and fear – or we can literally give ourselves some breathing space. Take in a few breaths. Exhale. And focus on what we need instead of what we've been striving to have."*[172]

Like Oprah we should resolve to be still and refuse to get flustered for as she says *"if you peel back the layers of your life – the frenzy, the noise – stillness is waiting"*.[173]

Tips for Practicing O'Habit #37 – Being still or refusing to get flustered:

- When confronted with an overwhelming situation ask yourself if becoming flustered will solve the problem. I can guarantee the answer would be no;

- Be still, talk to God about the problem and wait for direction.

O'Habit #38: Oprah Employs Vision

Vision without action is a dream. Action without vision is simply passing the time. Action with vision is making a positive difference.

Joel Barker

The most pathetic person in the world is someone who has sight, but has no vision.

Helen Keller

"*You are the only person alive who can see your big picture….*", says Oprah.[174] In fact, she talks about the fact that the only other person who shared her big picture and success was her friend Gayle King. Employing vision is something that Oprah has been doing since she was very young. At four years old while watching her mother stir a big black pot of boiling clothes she thought "*my life won't be like this…it will be better.*" And even when her grandmother would be wringing the chicken by the neck to prepare their next meal and invited her to "*watch me, 'cause you're going to have to learn how to do this*", Oprah thought "*don't need to watch Grandma because my life isn't going to be like this*". She knew exactly what she wanted from life and that is why when she was older and entered a beauty pageant she declared that she "*wanted to be a broadcast journalist because I believed in the truth. I was interested in proclaiming the truth to the world.*"[175]

Oprah is where she is today partly because of having vision. It is the one trait that can set you apart from everyone else. Dr. Myles Munroe says:

> *The greatest gift ever given to mankind is not the gift of sight, but the gift of vision. Sight is a function of the eyes; vision is a function of the heart. …Vision sets you free from the limitations of what the eyes can see and allows you to enter into the liberty of what the heart can feel. It is vision that makes the unseen visible and the unknown possible.*[176]

It was through the vision that moved Frederick W. Smith to draft a college paper on a proposal for overnight mail and despite obtaining a "C" grade and having his professor write on the paper in red "Do not dream of things that cannot happen", that I am able to send my parents in Maryland a fedex package that would leave Montserrat at 3pm and arrive by 10:30am the next day!

But as the opening quote of this chapter says "*vision without action is a dream*" and so we must let our actions be consistent with the vision we have for ourselves. While she may have never visualized herself as a talk show Queen, Oprah surely did things that supported her vision of better life. She enjoyed speaking and told People Weekly in a 1987 interview that she often "*made speeches to the cows.*"[177] As a teenager she was a member of the drama club and travelled to other schools for competitions as part of a combination speech and debate team.

Often times we tell ourselves we want to do this and we want to do that, yet we do not make our actions line up with our vision. At the age of sixteen I decided I wanted to become a lawyer, but not just any lawyer, but rather an "entertainment lawyer" – a niche that was foreign to the Caribbean at the time. I mapped out a plan and began taking steps that would allow me to achieve what seemed ridiculous. "An entertainment lawyer?", people would ask in amazement. "Who are you going to work for? Arrow?" Arrow was and is still to date the biggest thing in entertainment to come out of my island. He is the original performer of the famous tune "Hot Hot Hot" and is considered to be the King of Soca music. I enrolled at the Golden Gate University School of law and pursued a Masters in Intellectual Property and Entertainment law and, kept my vision at the forefront. Today, while I am based on the island of Montserrat I am referred to as an "entertainment lawyer" and I am consulted by entertainers and those in the creative industries on matters of intellectual property, all because I not only had a vision but I also put some action to it. And oh by the way, write your vision down.

In 1979 the graduates of the MBA program at Harvard were asked "Have you set clear written goals for your future and made plans to accomplish them?" Thirteen percent said they had goals but they were not written. A mere 3% said they had written down their goals and plans. In 1989, (ten years later) the same group was interviewed by the researchers and they found that the thirteen percent who had goals that were not written were earning on average twice as much as the 84 percent who had no goals at all. What was astounding was the fact that the 3 percent who had clear goals and had written their goals down were earning on average ten times as much as the other 97 percent of graduates all together.

Oprah is also known for writing her dreams down. In fact, when she met David Zaslav – CEO of Discovery Communications in 2007 who proposed a channel that would echo Oprah's "Live your Best Life" message, she was amazed. After listening to his proposal she got up from the meeting and said *"David come with me. I want to show you something."* Then she showed him some pages that she ripped from her 1992 journal where she had written down her vision of a television network dubbed "OWN i.e the Oprah Winfrey Network. She had found the pages in her desk drawer a few days before the meeting. She calls that moment *"Absolute divine order"*.

Where do you see yourself five years from now? What stirs you up that gives you overwhelming pleasure? What would you be doing if you won the lotto? Get a vision, write it down and get moving and while you are at it be inspired by Oprah who says that you should:

> *Move in the direction of your goal with all the force and verve you can muster-and then let go, releasing your plan to the power that's bigger than yourself and allowing your dream to unfold as its own masterpiece. Dream big, dream very big. Work hard-work very hard. And after you've done all you can, you can stand, wait, and fully surrender[178].*

Tips for Practicing O'Habit #38 – Developing or employing Vision:

- Get a Vision i.e create a mental picture of a future state;

- Write your vision down. In fact develop a detailed plan for your vision;

- Put your plan for your vision to action;

- Surround yourself with people who will support the vision.

O'Habit #39: Oprah Remembers her Spirit

We are not human beings on a spiritual journey. We are spiritual beings on a human journey.

Stephen R. Covey

Walk in the Spirit and you will not fulfill the desires of the flesh.

Galatians 5:16

Most of us have heard about "out of body experiences", "near to death encounters" and "the spirit realm", however, these are all things that remind us that we are spiritual beings. Oprah knows that very well and does what she could to remember her spirit and reminds us of the same thing. In her September 2009 "What I Know For Sure" column, she says, "*for me, there is no power without spiritual power.*"[179] So what then is the spirit? I believe that it is that part of us that transcends the physical realm and connects us with the unseen realm. What exactly does Oprah refer to as spirit or spirituality? According to her:

Spirituality is not religion. You can be spiritual and not have a religious context. The opposite is true too: You can be very religious with no spiritual dimension, just doctrine. Spirituality isn't something I believe in. It is what and who I am: a spiritual being having a human experience...[180]

Spirituality then is no organized religion that is thrust on us through doctrine and habit. Her efforts to remind us started in the mid-nineties when she began her "Remembering your Spirit" series – a segment that kept us aware that we were spirit as much as we were flesh. To this day she continues to remind us, writing in the May 2008 issue of her magazine:

Claiming my own spiritual depths and encouraging others to recognize the fullness of their potential through spiritual connection is my greatest purpose and calling. It's why I've continued to do the show these many years. [181]

What are we supposed to do with this knowledge that we are spirit indeed? Having been made aware that we are spirit what are we to do? Feed it! And every time we pray we feed our spirit. Every time we fast or give of ourselves so that the less fortunate can get a better life, we feed our spirit. In fact, whatever we do to deny the flesh nurtures our spirit which cannot be physically impaired. No wonder Oprah remembers her spirit and does all she can to grow spiritually sharing that she has "*read hundreds of books that have helped [her] become more spiritually attuned.*"[182] She also makes it her business to commune with spiritual gurus like Deepak Chopra and Eckhart Tolle for connecting with that realm of consciousness that releases the fullest potentiality of the individual. Besides appearances on her talk shows, she even organized online seminars to spread and share the messages of Eckhart Tolle, writer of "A New Earth".

Remember your spirit today by feeding and nurturing it. After all, at the end of the day, it's the only thing you have that will survive this earthly place.

Tips for Practicing O'Habit #39 – Remembering your Spirit:

- Feed your Spirit by giving, praying and fasting;

- Spend more time watching the channels on TV that facilitate spiritual growth such as TBN, and EWTN and less time watching shows that do nothing to uplift your spirit.

O'Habit #40: Oprah Adores Women and Especially Mothers

You don't love a woman because she's beautiful, but she is beautiful because you love her.

Unknown

A mother is not a person to lean on but a person to make leaning unnecessary.

Dorothy Canfield Fisher

Women are often described as the "*architects of our society*". There is no procreation without them and men the world over would be a lot more miserable. We in the western world take for granted the freedom we enjoy as it regards womanhood, while in some countries women are still considered unequal to men. Oprah adores women and especially mothers - and as a man who came from one, married to one and partook in the creation of two wonderful daughters, I can only commend her for that. Her love for women and mothers goes beyond the normal. Everything about Oprah screams "WOMAN". Her love and respect for women and mothers is magnified in the fact that she dedicated an entire issue of the Oprah Magazine to mothering. Several articles in the May 2006 issue addressed the theme and made women aware of discrimination based on parental responsibilities. Companies that hire and fire depending on whether you were pregnant or your likelihood to become pregnant were discussed and criticized. This is to be commended.

Her admiration for the female sex is not just lip service. When she decided to build a school in South Africa she meted out approximately forty million dollars towards the effort. The interesting thing was that the school was not just a school; it was a school just for girls. For Oprah "the girls" have been the center of her life. She speaks about them incessantly and treats them like princesses.

As for women who are mothers, the talk-show host holds them in high esteem calling them *"the greatest spiritual teachers in the world."*[183] and writes that:

> *We should no longer allow a mother to be defined as 'just a mom'. It is on her back that great nations are built. We should no longer allow any woman's voice to be drowned out or disregarded.*[184]

Her deep respect, love and admiration for woman and mothers have caused her to declare *"I'm in awe of good mothers..."*[185] Despite not being a mother herself and constantly telling her audience that she has no interest in becoming one, Oprah is in awe of good mothers. Her excuse for not being one was given in an interview with Diane Sawyer in May 2004. She explained that she could not have had the time to nurture children in Africa and elsewhere if she had been a mother, yet she holds mothers in high esteem.

Perhaps Oprah is trying to bring balance in a world where women are normally marginalized. Women are wonderful creations, and while the first one to walk this earth ate us out of a paradise, the world would be a better place if we hold them in higher esteem. And while I have no problem with that I believe it is somehow creating a void. A void that will later affect the society. This is why I am writing the next chapter....

Tips for Practicing O'Habit #40 – Adoring the women in your life:

- Take time out to honor the women in your life. Whether it is Mothers' Day or not send them flowers with a note to say how much you appreciate them;

- Support organizations that advance the cause for women;

- Treat younger women as if they are your sisters and older women as if they are your mother. This is actually a direct quote from the book of 1 Timothy chapter 5, verse 2.

O'Bad Habit!: The one Bad Habit Oprah Needs to Stop!

The process of raising money and climbing leadership's ladders that gets a man on the front pages requires a man to repress his fears, not express his fears. So a man's external story is visible; his internal story invisible.

Dr. Warren Farrell

When I was writing this book and announced to friends that I was writing a book, two questions would immediately follow. The first would be "what's the name of the book?" and having given them the title: O'Habits: 40 Success Habits of Oprah Winfrey and The One Bad Habit She needs to Stop!, the second question would immediately follow, "what's the bad habit?". Notwithstanding that I mentioned not 10, 20 or 30, but 40 success habits, everybody wanted to hear all about the "bad"! Most people want to accentuate the negative which I believe is wrong, but I am a supporter of Dale Carnegie's approach. He says that "*it is always easier to listen to unpleasant things after we have heard some praise about our good points*".[186]

I say all of that by way of introduction to say that I truly believe Oprah rocks!!! I adore her a great deal and have her as one of the four women in my life who I have a great deal of love and respect for (the other being my wife Cleo, my mother and Mrs. Verna Brandt who I refer to as my other mother). In fact Oprah inspired my television show 'The Warren Cassell Show". So to my family and close friends, it is shocking that I would even suggest Oprah has a bad habit. However, I want to say to you that if you have turned to this chapter as the first chapter you want to read, stop now! Go back and read all of the other chapters and then read this one.

As mentioned in the previous chapter, Oprah adores women and there is nothing wrong with that. However, her show, her magazine, the Oxygen network (that she co-founded), and the school (on which she spent in excess of forty million dollars) are exclusively geared towards women.

My criticism is, therefore, that Oprah focuses too much on the female sex and neglects to provide the same guidance and nurturing to the men with whom those women live. In fact, most times when men are involved in an episode of her show, it is subtly negative.

One blogger believes that thirty years ago women began speaking out on daytime talk-shows about the fact that men were making more money than they were. And when men were not speaking out, the women spoke about the fact that the men weren't speaking out.

The Oprah Winfrey Show and "O The Oprah Winfrey Magazine," in my opinion, fails to give men an adequate opportunity to speak out and let people know how they feel. In a sense then, I agree with the said blogger who blogged that:

> *When a daytime TV talk show allows women and girls, but not men and boys, to express their feelings about their own issues, it may reinforce the notion that in the personal sphere females' feelings and thoughts matter more. Or that males' feelings don't matter at all. It says to men, even to troubled or disturbed young boys, 'You, male, must tough it out on your own.'*[187]

That's the problem, men have been socialized to think that it isn't masculine to express their feelings, and that they always have to be tough. We need people to encourage men to speak out and to show emotions. Men also need to be nurtured. Further, they need to be taught how to be more sensitive, how to be better husbands to their wives and concerned fathers to their children.

Unfortunately, Oprah is not alone in excluding men. Even her sponsors are guilty of this. Dove, for example, is a "proud sponsor" of the show and during the advertisement boasts about how they are promoting self-esteem for girls. A self-esteem fund was even established by Dove; they boast that they have reached 3.5 million "female" lives so far and intend to reach 5 million by 2010. Their mission is about bolstering girls' self-esteem and their website features lots of little girls and women sharing how their self-esteem was boosted.

Interestingly enough, Dove claims that "*[f]or too long, beauty has been defined by stifling stereotypes. It's time to change all that....*" They seem to understand what "stifling stereotypes" are and I want to suggest that similar "stifling stereotypes" are crippling men. Kevin Cassell quotes Christina Hoff Sommers of the American Enterprise Institute in his article "Boys Falling Behind in US Education" says "*Girls in crisis? 'A myth' .... Just look at the statistics.... Boys 'dominate dropout lists, failure lists, and learning-disabilities lists.'*"[188]

Added to that, in a July 1, 2006 article: "The Problem With Boys", Tom Chiarella writing for Esquire magazine cautioned that "*[w]e've ignored all the evidence of male achievement and ambition deficits and stood aside as our sons have notched a growing record of failure and disengagement. It's time we did something about it. A call to action.*"

This is why I believe wholeheartedly that Oprah's all-girl school in Africa contributes to the intellectual "malercide" our boys. The girls attending have been given an excellent opportunity to learn in an environment where no educational material is lacking, leaving the boys behind. Furthermore, with this exclusion of boys I ask myself how are these girls taught to relate to the opposite sex? Given that they are being taught to socialize without the presence of the opposite sex, how will they react when they enter into a relationship with a man later in life? Can you imagine a graduate of Oprah's Academy growing up to be a brilliant and educated leader with an excellent career only to marry a dead beat young man who comes home daily to beat her mercilessly? Why was the academy only for girls?

While the statistics show that both genders performed better in single sex institutions when it came to academics, the single sex schools seem to weaken the overall social tapestry especially in places like Africa. Males are the ones who are in much need of guidance from an early age given their involvement in crime and social errors.

It's full time then, for Oprah to realize that her show can be a medium to not only emphasize female independence and importance of women, but to also re-educate all of us on the synergistic effect of men and women working together to create better tomorrows. Society cannot continue to promote the absence of men. We need to accept the weakness of both sexes and concentrate on the strengths and how those strengths can be used to support each other.

In the Fall of 2009, Oprah featured five women who were unknowingly dating the same man. They all came on the show to share their story with Oprah viewers. Not only were they fooled by this man, they all contracted HIV from him (the man is now serving a prison sentence in excess of forty years). I was saddened by the whole situation. Sad for the women involved and also, sad for the man. What was his experience growing up? Was he taught how to properly relate to the opposite sex? Was he neglected? Was there a defining moment in his life that caused him to have such disregard and lack of respect for women? These are the questions I asked myself after watching the episode because after all our lives are shaped by external factors.

Dr. Phil in his book Self Matters tells us that:

> *Social Scientists tell us that the entire origin of your self-concept, and therefore the determination of who you ultimately become in your life, can be traced to the events of a precious few days and the actions of an amazingly few key people involved in those happenings. I'm telling you that out of the thousands of days you have lived, out of the thousands and thousands of choices and decisions you have made, and out of all the thousands of people you have encountered, the basis of your entire life and who you have become can be boiled down to: Ten Defining Moments, Seven Critical Choices and Five Pivotal People.*[189]

I believe that the Oprah Winfrey Show could serve as a defining moment for many men. Moreover, Oprah herself can be one of the "pivotal persons" for many men. She has already served as a pivotal person for several women, and I think it's time she becomes that, generally, for men.

I am therefore suggesting to Oprah that she at least includes men in her philanthropic and educational thrust and especially since she's ending the show in 2011. You have done a great job in developing women and young ladies. I would like to invite you to have shows that will teach men how to be better sons, boyfriends and husbands. Since your show season is sometimes thematic why not an entire season to assist that group of people who I refer to as "the modern day weaker sex, men"? I am sure in the end it would make the women happier and create better communities for everyone. Given the limited time we have (only one season left), this is my "call to action"!

Suggestions for Oprah to stop the O'Bad Habit:\

- Dedicate the final season or at least a portion of it to developing better boys and men in our society. Some show ideas could include "Husbands of the Year", "How to Choose a Wife", "We're in this together", "Raising Boys to become Men". I claim no rights to these concepts and expect no reward;

- Whenever a show is being produced which is totally geared towards women, balance the show by obtaining a male perspective;

- Dedicate an entire issue of O The Oprah Magazine to men, not to bash them but to support them. Promote the issue beforehand and encourage women to buy the issue and give it to them as a gift. Perhaps this would be great for the month during which we celebrate father's day. After that issue, make a few pages geared towards men in every issue. So when they read it they would also read other pages. I can't understand why men do not read your magazine. I have learnt so much about how women think, what they want and what makes them happy from reading your magazine;

- Obtain the support of other celebrities to establish a similar school in Africa for boys modeled after the one you established for girls. Same objectives but targeted at boys.

END NOTES:

1   Brian Tracy, <u>Million Dollar Habits: Proven practices to Double and Triple your income</u>. Entrepreneur Press 2006, p. viii

2   Joel Olsteen, <u>Become a Better You – 7 Keys to Improving Your Life Every Day,</u> Free Press 2007, p. 198

3   Janet Rae Dupree, "Can You Become a Creature of New Habits?", The Oprah Magazine, January 2007, p. 165

4   Brian Tracy, <u>Million Dollar Habits: Proven practices to Double and Triple your income,</u> Entrepreneur Press, 2006, p. 36

5   Phil C. McGraw <u>Life Strategies: Doing what works, Doing what matters.</u> Hyperion,1999, p. 93

6   http://ecclesia.org/truth/40.html (accessed June 2008)

7   Rick Warren, The Purpose Driven Life, Zondervan p. 9

8   Rick Warren, The Purpose Driven Life, Zondervan p. 10

9   Stephen Galloway, "A Mighty Heart", Hollywood
      Reporter, December 2007, p. 10

10   Brian Tracy, <u>Million Dollar Habits: Proven practices
      to Double and Triple your income.</u> Entrepreneur Press
      2006, p.viii

11   Brian Tracy, <u>Million Dollar Habits: Proven Practices
      to Double and Triple Your Income</u>, Entrepreneur Press
      2006, p. 211

12   Dr. Mike Murdock, <u>Secrets of the Richest Man who Ever
      Lived</u>, Honor Books 1998, p. 123

13   Stephen Galloway, "A Mighty Heart", Hollywood
      Reporter, December 2007, p. 11

14   Dr. Mike Murdock, Secrets of the Richest Man who Ever
      Lived, Honor Books 1998, p. 127

15   Oprah Winfrey, "What I Know For Sure", The Oprah
      Magazine, November 2004, p. 298

16   Oprah Winfrey, "What I Know For Sure", The Oprah
      Magazine, November 2004, p. 298

17   Oprah Winfrey, "Unforgettable! Oprah's Top 20 Shows",
      The Oprah Magazine, October 2005, p. 281

18   Oprah Winfrey, "What I Know For Sure", The Oprah
      Magazine, May 2007 p. 378

19   John Mason, Imitation is Limitation, 2004 Bethany
      House, p. 104

20 Steve Purcell, "Oprah Opens School for Poor in South Africa", www.looktothestars.org (accessed September 13, 2009.

21 Joel Olsteen, Your Best Life Now, Warner Faith, 2004, p.221.

22 Oprah Winfrey, "What I Know For Sure", The Oprah Magazine, December 2005 WIKFS p. 332.

23 Stephen Galloway, "A Mighty Heart", Hollywood Reporter p. 10.

24 Amby Burfoot, "Inside Story", Runner's World, January 1995. p. 68

25 Christy Grosz and Stephen Galloway, "Leading Lady", Hollywood Reporter, December 2007, p. 19

26 David McLemore, "Oprah on Answering End of Questions at Beef Trial: She says Talkshow Was for Viewers, not Cattlemen," Dallas Morning News February 4, 1998, p. 1A.

27 Mark Babineck, Associated Press, February 26, 1998.

28 Quoted by Robert La Franco, "Piranha Is Good," Forbes, October 16, 1995, p. 66

29 The Oprah Winfrey Show 20th Anniversary Collection, Disc 3, (DVD)

30 J. Randy Taraborrelli, "How Oprah Does It All", Redbook, August 1996, p. 76

31 Oprah Winfrey, "What I Know For Sure" November 2004, p. 298

32 *The Oprah Winfrey Show 20ᵗʰ Anniversary DVD,* Disc 6.

33 *The Oprah Winfrey Show 20ᵗʰ Anniversary DVD,* Disc 6.

34 http://www.laughteryoga.us/laughter-yoga-oprah-winfrey.php (accessed October 17, 2009).

35 http://www.farmersalmanac.com/natural_cures/a/laughter-the-best-medicine-of-all (Accessed October 17, 2009).

36 http://www.wholefamily.com/aboutteensnow/feelings/lighten_up/laughter.html (accessed October 16, 2009).

37 "What I know for Sure", O The Oprah Magazine, July 2006 p. 224.

38 Alan Ebert, "Oprah Winfrey Talks Openly about Oprah," Good Housekeeping, September 1991, p. 62.

39 Matthew Flamm, "Book 'em, Oprah," Entertainment Weekly, October 25, 1998.

40 "Oprah Donates $100,000 to Harold Washington Library," Jet, October 7, 1991, p. 18.

41 Pamela Gien, "Building a Dream," O The Oprah Magazine, January, 2007 p. 158.

42 Pamela Gien, "Building a Dream," O The Oprah Magazine, January, 2007 p. 158.

43 Oprah Winfrey, "What I Know For Sure," O The Oprah Magazine, July 2006.

44 Brian Tracy, "How to Master Your Time" (Audio), Tape 6.

45 "Oprah Winfrey, Unforgettable! Oprah's Top 20 Shows," O The Oprah Magazine, October 2005.

46   John R. Dijulis, <u>Secret Service: Hidden systems that Deliver Unforgettable Customer Service,</u> 2003 American Management Association (AMACOM) p. 111.)

47   *Bob Nelson,* <u>1001 Ways to Reward Employees</u>, Workman Publishing, Introduction.

48   The Oprah Winfrey Show 20th Anniversary DVD, Disc 6.

49   The Oprah Winfrey Show 20th Anniversary DVD, Disc 6.

50   Oprah Winfrey, "What I Know For Sure," O The Oprah Magazine, January 2006 p. 188.

51   Anne Kirrin – Benefits of having a dog, http://www.all-small-dog-breeds.com/Articles/Article-Benefits-of-having-a-dog.htm

52   Anne Kirrin – Benefits of having a dog, http://www.all-small-dog-breeds.com/Articles/Article-Benefits-of-having-a-dog.htm

53   Oprah Winfrey, "What I Know For Sure," O The Oprah Magazine, June 2009, p. 209.

54   Oprah Winfrey, "Here We Go", O The Oprah Winfrey Magazine, June 2009, p. 27.

55   Janet Sternburg, "Oprah's Secret Garden", O At Home, Spring 2008, p. 82.

56   "Our Best Decorating Ideas ever", Oprah Winfrey Show, Harpo 1996.

57   Janet Sternburg, "Oprah's Secret Garden", O At Home, Spring 2008, p. 83.

58   when asked why he had a team of twenty-one assistants.

59   The Oprah Winfrey Show 20th Anniversary Collection,
      disc 6 (DVD).

60   Dr. Mike Murdock, <u>Secrets of the Richest Man who ever
      Lived</u>, Honor Books p. 92.

61   Dr. Myles Munroe, <u>The Principles and Power of Vision:
      Keys to achieving personal and corporate destiny</u>,
      Whitaker House, 2003, p. 151.

62   The Oprah Winfrey Show 20th Anniversary Collection,
      disc 5 (DVD).

63   Robert Morris, <u>The Power of Your Words</u>, Regal, 2006,
      p. 28.

64   Dr. Cindy Trimm, <u>What Have You Put in the
      Atmosphere?</u>, Cindy Trimm Ministries, (Audio).

65   http://www.managementstudyguide.com/delegation_of_
      authority.htm (accessed October 12, 2009.

66   A day in the life of Oprah, 20th Anniversary Collection,
      2005, Disc 6 (Audio).

67   "A day in the life of Oprah", 20th Anniversary Collection,
      2005, Disc 6 (Audio).

68   The Oprah Winfrey Show 20th Anniversary Collection,
      disc 6 (DVD).

69   http://ezinearticles.com/?The-Importance-of-
      Delegation&id=192169 (accessed October 12, 2009).

70 Colin Cowie, "A Party from the Heart", People, May 30 2005, p. 112.

71 Dr. Mike Murdock, Secrets of the Richest Man who ever Lived, 1998, Honor Books p. 89.

72 Helen S. Garson, Oprah Winfrey: a Biography, Greenwood Press, 2004, p. 95.

73 Oprah Winfrey, "TV's Super Women," ladies Home Journal, March 1988, p. 167.

74 Judy Markey, "Brassy, Sassy Oprah Winfrey," Cosmopolitan, September 1986, p. 98.

75 Oprah Winfrey, "Unforgettable! Oprah's Top 20 shows", O The Oprah Magazine, October 2005, p. 280.

76 Stormie Omartian, The Power of a Praying Husband, Harvest House, 2001, p. 88.

77 "Oprah talks to Elizabeth Edwards", O The Oprah Magazine: June 2009 p. 154.

78 Oprah Winfrey "Here We Go", O The Oprah Magazine, February 2003, p. 33.

79 Garry North, "The Horror of being Oprah", http://www.lewrockwell.com/north/north174.html.

80 Oprah Winfrey, "What I Know For Sure", O The Oprah Magazine, May 2007, p. 378.

81 Oprah on Oprah Live, Season 24, Friday November 20, 2009 during an interview with Ray Romano.

82   Oprah Winfrey, "What I Know For Sure", O The *Oprah Magazine, September 2002, p. 294.*

83   Jennifer Harris and Elwood Watson, "Introduction: Oprah Winfrey as a Subject and Spectacle", The Oprah Phenomenon, p. 9.

84   Oprah Winfrey 20th Anniversary Collection DVD, Disc 1.

85   Oprah Winfrey, "What I Know For Sure", O The *Oprah Magazine, August 2001.*

86   Oprah and Gayle Uncensored", The Oprah Magazine, August 2006 p. 246.

87   James Merritt, "Friends", Audio CD.

88   Dr. Myles Munroe p. 158.

89   Dr. Myles Munroe, The Principles and Power of Vision, Whitaker House, 2003, p. 158.

90   Lisa Kogan, "Oprah and Gayle Uncensored", O The Oprah Magazine, August 2006, p. 188.

91   Lisa Kogan, "Oprah and Gayle Uncensored", O The Oprah Magazine, August 2006, p. 188.

92   Oprah Winfrey, "What I Know for Sure", O The Oprah Magazine, August 2006, p. 254.

93   Sonia Alleyene, "Oprah Means Business", Black Enterprise, June 2008, p. 122.

94   Sonia Alleyene, "Oprah Means Business", Black Enterprise, June 2008, p. 122.

95   Christy Grosz and Stephen Galloway, "Leading Lady", Hollywood Reporter, December 2007, p. 19.

96   The Oprah Winfrey Show 20th Anniversary collection, disc 1 (DVD).

97   Oprah Winfrey, "What I Know For Sure", O The Oprah Magazine, September 2009 p. 232.

98   *Delatorro McNeal II,* Caught Between a Dream and a Job: How to Leave the 9-to-5 and Step Into the Life You've Always Wanted, Excel Books 2008, p. 20.

99   Mary South "What Do You Really Want to Do With Your Life?", O The Oprah Magazine, September 2007, p. 303.

100   Http://www.wisdomquotes.com/000857.html (accessed October 11, 2009).

101   Oprah Winfrey, "What I Know For Sure", Oprah Magazine, July 2007.

102   As quoted by Shawna Malcolm, "Oprah Winfrey: The best Friend Popular Culture Ever Had," Entertainment Weekly, November 11, 1999.

103   Joyce Myer, Approval Addiction: Overcoming Your Need to Please Everyone, Warner Faith, 2005 p. 164.

104   Oprah Winfrey, "What I Know For Sure," O The Oprah Magazine, October 2005, p. 350.

105   Oprah Winfrey, "Here We Go," O The Oprah Magazine, January 2003, p. 21.

106   Oprah Winfrey, "Here We Go," O The Oprah Magazine, December 2003,

107 Marcia Z. Nelson, <u>The Gospel According to Oprah</u>, Westminster John Knox Press 2005, p.29,

108 Marcia Z. Nelson, <u>The Gospel According to Oprah</u>, Westminster John Knox Press, 2005, pp. 32-33.

109 John Mason, <u>Imitation is Limitation</u>, 2004, Bethany House p. 153.

110 Brain Tracy, <u>Million Dollar Habits: Proven Practices to Double and Triple Your Income</u>, Entrepreneur Press p. 193.

111 Phillip C. McGraw, PH.D, <u>Life's Strategies: Doing What Works, Doing What Matters</u>, Hyperion, 1999, p. 201.

112 Marcia Z. Nelson, <u>The Gospel According to Oprah</u>, Westminster John Knox Press, p.77.

113 Will Smith "Freakin It" from the Will 2K album"

114 Oprah Winfrey, 20th Anniversary Collection, Disc 1.

115 Robert Le Franco, "Piranha is Good," Forbes, October 16, 1995, p. 66.

116 Stephen Galloway, "A Mighty Heart", Hollywood Reporter, December 2007, p. 14.

117 Oprah Winfrey, "What I Know For Sure", O The Oprah Magazine, January 2003 p. 164.

118 Stormie Omartian, <u>Greater Health God's Way</u>, Harvest House, 1996, p. 111.

119 Oprah Winfrey, "What I Know For Sure", O The Oprah Magazine, June 2006, p. 284.

120 Stormie Omartian, <u>Greater Health God's Way</u>, Harvest House 1996, p. 116.

121 Oprah Winfrey, "What I Know For Sure", O The Oprah Magazine, June 2006, p. 284.

122 Stormie Omartian, <u>Greater Health God's Way</u>, Harvest House, 1996, pp. 24-25.

123 Oprah Winfrey, "What I Know For Sure", The Oprah Magazine, August 2004, p. 222.

124 Oprah Winfrey, "What I Know For Sure", The Oprah Magazine, August 2005, p. 244.

125 Gary Zukav during an episode of The Oprah Winfrey Show on Authentic Power in 2000.

126 *Dr. Myles Munroe, <u>Principles and Power of Vision: Keys to achieving personal and corporate destiny</u>, Whitaker House, 2003* p. 152.

127 Ibid p. 158.

128 Ibid p. 158.

129 Marcia Z. Nelson, <u>The Gospel According to Oprah</u>, 2005, Westminster John Knox Press, p. 49.

130 Larry King, <u>How to Talk to Anyone, Anytime, Anywhere: The Secrets of Good Communication,</u> 1994, Crown Publishers Inc., p. 41.

131 Oprah Winfrey, "What I Know For Sure", O The Oprah Magazine, April 2004, p.254.

132 "Oprah Winfrey's Success Story," Ladies Home Journal, March 1987 p. 64.

133 "Oprah Winfrey's Success Story," Ladies Home Journal, March 1987 p. 64.

134 Richard Zoglin, "Lady with a Calling," Time, August 8, 1988, p. 62.

135 Dr. Mike Murdock, <u>Secrets of the Richest Man Who Ever Lived</u> by Mike Murdock, 1998 Honor Books, pp. 69-70.

136 Oprah Winfrey, "What I Know For Sure" O The Oprah Winfrey Magazine, April 2004 p. 254.

137 Ivenia Benjamin, <u>Seeds of Sacrifice, Harvests of Faith</u>, Emmanuel Publications 2005 p. 52.

138 Linded Gross, "Oprah Winfrey, Wonder Woman," Ladies' Home Journal, December 1988, p. 40.

139 Brian Tracy, <u>Million dollar Habits: Proven Power Practices to Double and Triple Your Income</u>, 2006, Entrepreneur Press, p. 50.

140 The Oprah Winfrey Show 20th Anniversary Collection, Disc 6 (DVD).

141 Mike Murdock, <u>Secrets of the Richest Man Who Ever Lived</u>, Honor Books p. 71.

142 Oprah Winfrey, "Reserve, Restore, Take Sundays Off… Oprah Energy Policy", The Oprah Magazine, July 2003, p. 139.

143 Brian Tracy, Newsletter to Subscribers to briantracy.com sent February 13, 2005.

144 Dale Carnegie, <u>How to Stop Worrying and Start Living</u>, 1984 Pocket Books, p. 235.

145 Oprah Winfrey, "What I Know For Sure", O The Oprah Magazine, April 2004, p. 254.

146 Stormie Omartian, <u>Greater Health God's Way</u>, Harvest House 1996, p. 249.

147 Title 53 – Sundays, Holidays and Other special days. Section 53-1-40.

148 Oprah Winfrey, "What I Know For Sure", O The Oprah Magazine, April 2004, p. 254

149 Stephen Galloway, "A Mighty Heart", Hollywood Reporter, December 2007, p. 11.

150 John Mason, <u>Know Your Limits then Ignore them</u>, Insight Publishing Group, 1999, p. 35.

151 Christy Grosz and Stephen Galloway, "Leading Lady", The Hollywood Reporter, Dec 2007 p. 20.

152 Oprah Winfrey, "What I Know For Sure", O The Oprah Magazine, July 2003. p. 186.

153 Oprah Winfrey, "What I know For Sure", O The Oprah Magazine, January 2007.

154 Oprah Winfrey, "What I know For Sure", The Oprah Magazine, January 2007.

155 Oprah Winfrey, "What I Know For Sure", O The Oprah Magazine, January 2007.

156   Oprah Winfrey, "Here We Go", O The Oprah Magazine, May 2003, p. 43.

157   Oprah Winfrey, "Here We Go", O The Oprah Magazine, May 2003, p. 43.

158   Oprah Winfrey, 32, "The Exception That Proves the Rule in Talk Show Hosts," People Weekly, August 25, 1986, p. 69.

159   Oprah Winfrey, "What I Know For Sure," O The Oprah Magazine, September 2003, p. 286.

160   Donald Trump and Bill Zanker, Think Big and Kick Ass!, Collins, 2007 p. 47.

161   Dr. Myles Munroe, The Principles and Power of Vision, Whitaker house 2003, p. 109.

162   Oprah Winfrey, "What I Know For Sure," O The Oprah Magazine, September 2003, p. 286.

163   Stephen Galloway, "A Mighty Heart", Hollywood Reporter, December 2007, p. 10.

164   Christy Grosz and Stephen Galloway, "Leading Lady", Hollywood Reporter, December 2007 p. 20.

165   Oprah Winfrey, "What I Know For Sure", O The Oprah Magazine, March 2006, p. 286.

166   Sonia Alleyne, "Oprah Means Business", Black Enterprise, June 2008, p.117

167   Sonia Alleyne, "Oprah Means Business", Black Enterprise, June 2008, p. 124.

168 Oprah Winfrey, "What I Know For Sure", O The Oprah Magazine, March 2006, p. 286.

169 Oprah Winfrey, What I Know For Sure" O The Oprah Magazine, October 2006 p. 376.

170 Oprah Winfrey, "What I Know for Sure", O The Oprah Magazine, May 2009, p. 224.

171 Catherine Ponder, The Prospering Power of Prayer", DeVorss Publications, 1983, p.22.

172 Oprah Winfrey, "What I Know For Sure", O The Oprah Magazine, May 2009 p. 224.

173 Oprah Winfrey, "What I Know For Sure", The Oprah Magazine, May 2006 p. 310.

174 Oprah Winfrey, "What I Know For Sure", O The Oprah Magazine, September, 2002 p. 294.

175 "Oprah Winfrey Interview, February 1991," Academy of Achievement, Museum of Living History, ww.achievement.org/autodoc/page/win0int-2 (October 25, 2004).

176 Dr. Myles Munroe, The Principles and Power of Vision, Whitaker House 2003 p. 11.

177 Alan Richman, "Oprah," People Weekly, January 12, 1987, p. 50.

178 *Oprah Winfrey, "What I Know For Sure", O The Oprah Magazine, September 2002,* p. 294.

179 Oprah Winfrey, "What I Know For Sure", O The Oprah Magazine, September 2009 p. 232.

180 Oprah Winfrey, "What I Know For Sure", O The Oprah Magazine, May 2008 p. 348.

181 Oprah Winfrey, "What I Know For Sure", O The Oprah Magazine, May 2008 p. 348.

182 Oprah Winfrey, "What I Know For Sure", O The Oprah Magazine, May 2008 p. 348.

183 "Unforgettable! Oprah Top 20 Shows, O The Oprah Magazine, October 2005 p. 282.

184 Oprah Winfrey, "What I Know For Sure", O The Oprah Magazine, May 2003 p. 290.

185 Oprah Winfrey, "What I Know For Sure", O The Oprah Magazine, May 2003 p. 290.

186 Dale Carnegie, <u>How to Win Friends and Influence people,</u> 1936, Pocket Books p.193.

187 http://battlinbog.blog-city.com/a_letter_to_dr_phil_on_the_sexes.htm

188 http://www.kevincassell.com/blog/index.php?id=19 (Accessed October 31 2009)

189 Dr. Phil McGraw, Ph.D, <u>Self Matters: Creating your Life From the Inside Out</u>, Simon & Schuster, 2001, p.90

BUY A SHARE OF THE FUTURE IN YOUR COMMUNITY

These certificates make great holiday, graduation and birthday gifts that can be personalized with the recipient's name. The cost of one S.H.A.R.E. or one square foot is $54.17. The personalized certificate is suitable for framing and will state the number of shares purchased and the amount of each share, as well as the recipient's name. The home that you participate in "building" will last for many years and will continue to grow in value.

Here is a sample SHARE certificate:

HABITAT FOR HUMANITY

THIS CERTIFIES THAT
YOUR NAME HERE
HAS INVESTED IN A HOME FOR A DESERVING FAMILY

1985-2005
TWENTY YEARS OF BUILDING FUTURES IN OUR
COMMUNITY ONE HOME AT A TIME

1200 SQUARE FOOT HOUSE @ $65,000 = $54.17 PER SQUARE FOOT
This certificate represents a tax deductible donation. It has no cash value.

YES, I WOULD LIKE TO HELP!

I support the work that Habitat for Humanity does and I want to be part of the excitement! As a donor, I will receive periodic updates on your construction activities but, more importantly, I know my gift will help a family in our community realize the dream of homeownership. I would like to SHARE in your efforts against substandard housing in my community! (Please print below)

PLEASE SEND ME _____ SHARES at $54.17 EACH = $ $_____

In Honor Of: _____

Occasion: (Circle One)   HOLIDAY   BIRTHDAY   ANNIVERSARY

       OTHER: _____

Address of Recipient: _____

Gift From: _____ *Donor Address:* _____

Donor Email: _____

I AM ENCLOSING A CHECK FOR $ $_____ PAYABLE TO HABITAT FOR HUMANITY OR PLEASE CHARGE MY VISA OR MASTERCARD *(CIRCLE ONE)*

Card Number _____ Expiration Date: _____

Name as it appears on Credit Card _____ Charge Amount $ _____

Signature _____

Billing Address _____

Telephone # Day _____ Eve _____

PLEASE NOTE: Your contribution is tax-deductible to the fullest extent allowed by law.
Habitat for Humanity • P.O. Box 1443 • Newport News, VA 23601 • 757-596-5553
www.HelpHabitatforHumanity.org

CPSIA information can be obtained at www.ICGtesting.com
Printed in the USA
BVOW04s0329300914

368872BV00001B/31/P